GANDHI IN CURRENT PERSPECTIVE

GANDHI IN CURRENT PERSPECTIVE

RAVINDRA KUMAR

GYAN

Gandhi in Current Perspective

ISBN: 978-81-212-1179-6

Published in 2013 in India by
Gyan Publishing House
23, Main Ansari Road, Daryaganj,
New Delhi - 110002
Phones : 23282060, 23261060
Fax : (011) 23285914
E-mail : books@gyanbooks.com
Website: gyanbooks.com

Laser Typesetting by: Dinesh Kumar, Delhi

Printed at: G. Print Process, Delhi

Dedicated

To

All Those

Fighting Non-violently

For

Freedom and Equality

In

Asia and Africa

Contents

Foreword

Non-violence is an ideal of human civilization. However, throughout history it has remained ideal and has hardly been put to practice, particularly in political practice. War has been the norm rather than non-violence. Many saints and *Rishis* exhorted rulers for peace, but mostly in vain. Buddhism and Jainism, the two great Indian religions emphasized compassion and non-killing, but their history is also not devoid of violence.

Agreeing to Dr. Ravindra Kumar's view that ***"shattering centuries old myth that non-violence was a subject limited to hermits and cave-dwellers, Gandhiji used non-violence in the political sphere and proved that it could be successfully applied in all walks of life and at all levels - individual to international - so long as the applier's intention is clear and full of honesty"***, I am also of the opinion that Mahatma Gandhi is the only exception, not only in India, but in world history, who could devise an effective political tool to practice non-violence [*Ahimsa*] and he could humble the most powerful of the empires of his time, the British Empire. It was not a small achievement. Many of his colleagues also thought it to be impossible. But Gandhiji wedded it to truth and truth has its own power. In the words of Gandhiji himself, "***The Truth is far more powerful than any weapon of mass destruction.***"

It should be noted that non-violence by itself and devoid of truth has no meaning. To Quote Gandhiji again, ***"My religion is based on truth and non-violence. Truth is my God. Non-violence is the means of realizing Him."*** Obviously, if non-violence is a body, truth is its spirit, its life. It is common knowledge that politics is usually based on interests, but Mahatma Gandhi based it on truth and elevated truth to divinity as is categorically evident from his own statement mentioned above. Then only this could become possible. It should also be noted that truth is possible only if life is need based and not greed based. Gandhiji adopted starkly simple life style in order to enforce regimen of truth.

Thus, there are three ingredients of philosophy of non-violence –truth, simplicity and non-violence and in ultimate analysis non-violence is product of truth and simple need – based life style. Mahatma Gandhi was highly creative in his approach. He adopted spinning wheel from rural India to demonstrate simplicity. This spinning wheel served two purposes –it became symbol of simplicity and also symbol of employment when the British imported goods were threatening our rural economy.

Gandhiji kept on experimenting with the forms of non-violence and nothing was final for him. He evolved new concepts and tools. And what is more important for the pluralist world today is that Mahatma Gandhi, though intensely religious was not ritualistic, but spiritual and value-based and, hence, could borrow from different religions without hesitation. He could proclaim that he is a Hindu as well as a Muslim, a Christian, a Buddhist, a Sikh and a Jain. This universal spiritual outlook knocked off the very basis of inter-religious violence and promoted non-violence.

Much can be written on Gandhiji's philosophy of non-violence and its relevance can never be lost in our violent world. I congratulate Dr. Ravindra Kumarji for writing this timely and useful book. He is very much Gandhian in his approach and this book will be of great use for students of Gandhian philosophy as today some people are glorifying themselves by invoking name of Gandhi even those who are most un–Gandhian like.

Dr. Asghar Ali Engineer

Introduction

In the issue of the Harijan of April 29, 1933, Mahatma Gandhi wrote, ***"I would like to say to the diligent reader of my writings and to others who are interested in them that I am not at all concerned with appearing to be consistent. In my search after Truth I have discarded many ideas and learnt many new things. Old as I am in age, I have no feeling that I have ceased to grow inwardly or that my growth will stop at the dissolution of the flesh. What I am concerned with is my readiness to obey the call of Truth, my God, from moment to moment, and, therefore, when anybody finds any inconsistency between any two writings of mine, if he has still faith in my sanity, he would do well to choose the later of the two on the same subject."***

From the above statement it is well evident that the Mahatma had accepted the eternality of the law of change; he was always for accepting it in his ideas and actions, both. Further, he supported for the refinement in ideas and stressed on adopting them in prevailing circumstances of space. Only this single distinctiveness is sufficient enough to prove the significance of Gandhi's ideas in current perspective, and it will be so in the times to come.

Having this uniqueness as the nuclei, I have had opportunities to speak in various universities and institutions of higher learning in India and abroad during the last two years. The manuscript of the present volume entitled, *Gandhi in Current Perspective* is in fact has been prepared from the selected speeches I have delivered there and among them my address on *Gandhian Non-Violence in Current Perspectives*, now a chapter of this manuscript, is of particular mention. The other speeches in the form of included chapters comprise of *Global Peace Movement and Relevance of Gandhian View*, *A Civil Society of Gandhi's Imagination*, *Gandhian View of Civilization*, *Education and Peace: With Reference to Gandhian Viewpoint* and *Gandhian Concept of Woman-Education: An Analysis*.

Some of the chapters included in this manuscript may seem new to the present generation. But inclusion of these chapters should be considered important for the youths of today as it brings into light the untouched aspects of Gandhian philosophy. The Mahatma had always held the young people in high esteem. Recognizing the role and contribution of youths in nation's building, he once went to the extent of saying, ***"Young men...claiming...to be the father of tomorrow, should be the salt of the nation. If the saltloses its flavour wherewith shall it be salted?"***

I believe that the readers will find this publication very interesting. Through this they will be able to comprehend the commitment of the Mahatma to the law of change and his call for accepting ideas in their refined form as per the demand of time and space.

I am thankful to Dr. Kiran Lata Dangwal and Mr. Sachin Arora for reading proofs of this manuscript with extra care.

Ravindra Kumar

1
Gandhian Non-Violence in Current Perspectives

"Non-violence is not a rough thing as it has been enunciated. Undoubtedly, it is a part of non-violence to abstain from hurting some living being, but it is only an iota pertaining to its identity. The principle of non-violence is also shattered by every evil thought, false utterance, hatred or wishing something bad unto someone. It is also shattered per possession of necessary worldly things."

-MK Gandhi

"To cause pain or wish ill to or to take the life of any living being out of a danger or a selfish intent is Himsa. On the other hand after a calm and clean judgment to kill or cause pain to living being with a view to its spiritual or physical benefit from a pure, selfless intent may be the purest form of Ahimsa. Each such case must be judged individually and on its own merits. The final test as its violence or non-violence is after all the intent underlying the act." –MK Gandhi

Gandhi's above statement is self-explanatory to clarify his viewpoint pertaining to *Ahimsa* [non-violence]. Besides, it is sufficient enough to elucidate significance of Gandhian concept of *Ahimsa* on the one hand and its adaptability on the other. Furthermore, it is fully capable to prove the uniqueness and excellence of *Ahimsa* in the current perspective. Above all, it may serve as a guide to those who opt for *Ahimsa* in its refined form under prevailing situations of time in future.

How? In this context, it is feasible to acquire familiarity with the word-meaning of non-violence, and simultaneously, with its foremost concepts prior to attempt any critical analysis.

Word Meaning

Non-violence is constituted by the two words: *non* and *violence*. The former, *non,* is a prefix which, after its use with a word, simply explains negative or opposite state of the word concerned. In my opinion nothing more is required to append or explain the role of the concept.

The term *violence* is derived from the Latin word *violare* [present participle *violans*], and its root may be traced to the Latin words *vis* [force] and *fero* [to carry].[1] On basis of the generally accepted explanation of above-mentioned terms [*vis* and *fero*] violence could be interpreted as *to do something by force*. The currently prevalent English word violence is itself observed in terms of expression of physical or verbal force against self or other. It is synonymous to a compelling action against one's will.[2]

The notion of *violence* has been variously defined and explained by scholars, thinkers and philosophers of repute, from time-to-time. As almost all such explanations are available for analysis, I do not deem it vital to say anything further in this regard except that non-violence is a state just opposed to violence.

The Indian Etymology

According to the Indian etymology *Ahimsa* [non-violence] comprises of the following three elements:

- A [अ];
- *Hims* [हिंस]; and
- A [अ]

Like the English word *non*, *A* [अ] in Indian parlance also conveys the negative state of the concerned word. Plainly speaking, after its [अ] placement as prefix to a word the opposite connotation of the word becomes apparent. For example: *Asahayog*, *Asvikar* or *Amaryaadit*.

Hims [हिंस] as is evident, again with [अ] [as a nominal

suffix] divulges the state of *Himsa* [violence], i.e., an act of causing pain to others, and spoiling life in any form.

Since ancient times the Indian scholars have been elaborating upon *Himsa* [violence] comprehensively. More specifically they have been analyzing it minutely from the word-meaning perspective. Based upon these explanations and analysis of *Himsa* [violence], they have also been striving to define *Ahimsa* [non-violence]. All such explanations and analysis are available. Particularly interpretations regarding word meaning of *Ahimsa* are well before us to urge and encourage reanalyzing and reinterpreting them according to the demand of time and prevailing conditions of space, and preferably on the basis of the fundamental spirit in the root of *Ahimsa*.

Main Concepts

Consequently many excellent, unique and worthy concepts of non-violence have developed from time-to-time, both in the East and the West. Most of the concepts developing in the East relate to India. The importance of *Ahimsa* as a supreme human value has been explained by Indian scholars and thinkers. Since ancient times they have analyzed it minutely with the sole purpose of inspiring people to make it the basis of their day-to-day practices, because despite existence, prosperity and peace in life are possible only through continuous practices of non-violence.[3] Therefore, having the East, and particularly Asia in the centre, discussing the main Indian concepts relating to *Ahimsa* first, will not be out of context.

Indian View

Ahimsa occupies its due place in philosophies related to all the four major Indian religious-communities -Hindu [*Vedic*], Jain, Buddhist and Sikh. In fact, *Ahimsa* has been placed there in the highest esteem as the supreme human value. Not only this, since ancient times *Ahimsa* has been playing a vital role in the lives of followers of religious-communities like Hindu-[*Vedic*], Jain and Buddhist. In an all-inclusive manner it can be said that non-violence has been the central point in day-to-day practices of almost all Indians. Hence, emergence of exemplary concepts pertaining to *Ahimsa* in the basic philosophies of all the four religious-communities [or as generally said religions] in which, as known to all of us, three[4] are ancient while one[5] was established some five centuries ago, due to their uniqueness, they necessitate a brief analysis.

Vedic [Hindu] Philosophy

The *Vedas* are the fountain of that philosophy, which is popularly known as Hinduism today. The *Vedas*[6] are the oldest religious treatises of the world. And in my opinion *Ahimsa*, as a supreme human value, is established in all of them in general and in the *Rigveda* in particular. Perhaps many of us may not be aware of the fact that *Ahimsa* along with the principle of Universalism and Human Unity emerges in the first *Shloka* of first *Sukta* of the first *Mandala* of the *Rigveda*.[7] However, it is a different matter if prayers to God [or gods] were the chief basis for desiring *Ahimsa* at the time of composition of the *Vedas* and particularly the *Rigveda* in prevailing situations, and spiritualism was the main source of realizing non-violence.

Besides the *Rigveda*, in the other three *Vedas* [the *Yajurveda*, the *Samveda* and the *Atharvaveda*] also *Ahimsa* appears as a keen desire for affability with fellow beings, fearlessness, and release from grieves and injuries.[8]

In the treatises of the later period, particularly the *Upanishads*, the *Manusmriti* and *Srimadbhagvadgita*, *Ahimsa* clearly appears as a *Dharma*, *Jnana* [knowledge], *Satya* [truth], a sense of duty and the supreme human value. The conclusion that we can draw from all mentions in the *Vedas* and other *Vedic* literature about the concept of *Ahimsa* is that it implies ***'not to injure and not to kill an innocent living being is non-violence'*** and thus, ***'complete abstinence from violence is non-violence'***. Moreover, *Ahimsa* must be an essential part of human behaviour. A human being should be non-violent in theory and practice, both. And, finally non-violence should be there as the basic spirit in the root of his every act.

Jainism

The concept of *Ahimsa* in Jainism is undoubtedly unique and extraordinary. Here it is more dominant in comparison to other Indian concepts relating to it. Moreover, it is completely based upon the negative aspect of violence as is evident from a brief statement, in which it has been said that ***"nahimsa ahimsa."***[9]

Jainism, as is well known, intrinsically revolves around *Ahimsa*. Non-violence is accepted as *Brahman* there. The scope of the concept of *Ahimsa* under Jainism is so comprehensive that it includes not causing even superfluous diversion of nature besides aversion from the slightest violence towards the tiniest living creature. A human being is expected to strictly follow the principle of *Ahimsa* realizing the spirit in the root of the following *Shloka*:

"Ahimsa Savvasattanam Sada Nivvekarika, Ahimsa Savvasattesu Param Bambhamani D iyam "[10]

Meaning thereby: ***"Non-violence, very dear to all living beings, is pacifying; is Brahman."***

Therefore, keeping the perception of ***"atmavat sarvabhuteshu"***[11] firmly in mind one must follow the principle of ***"parasparopgraho jivanam"***[12], and thus should come forward to cooperate with others.

Along with any kind of violence, a killing by mistake [or knowingly/unknowingly] is equally accountable in Jainism. It is a subject of reckoning. For, a human being is liable to blame. In this regard the following explanation of a verse from one of the *Jain Sutras* is adequate for corroboration:

"The Arhatas and Bhagvatas of the past and present, and future, all say thus, speak thus, declare thus, explain thus: all breathing, existing, living sentient creatures should not be slain, nor treated with himsa, nor tormented, nor driven away."

Just from the short statement, ***"nor driven away"***, it is evident that the concept of *Ahimsa* in Jainism is really severe. Moreover, Jainism's laying great stress on self-sacrifice, self-control and discipline makes its concept of non-violence intricate and rather difficult for common people to follow it. That is why; despite its being unique, its having based on negative aspect of violence, it is difficult to be accomplished by each and every one.

Buddhism

Although like Jainism, the concept of *Ahimsa* in Buddhism is also connected to self-control and discipline, [14] and to a large extent, with the unique principle of "***parasparopgraho jivanam***",[15] but, neither Buddhism and nor Gautama Buddha himself brings non-violence within the scope of superfluous rigidity. Despite accepting *Ahimsa* as the supreme human value[16] and declaring it to be the most precious jewel of humanity, Buddhism lays great stress on its practical aspects so that it could be feasible to common man. That is why; Buddhism calls for making *Ahimsa* an indivisible part of day-to-day human practices in its refined form as per the demand of time.

During the lifetime of Buddha, *Karuna*, i.e., compassion [union of pity and friendliness] was the best and practical reflection of non-violence. It was loving kindness towards all beings [*Metta*]. Moreover, it was itself a dimension of the theory of *Ahimsa* on the one hand, and recognition to the right to live of each and every living being on the other. Besides being an acid test of humanity, it was also the acceptability of principles of love and protection of life. Moreover, it symbolized the revelation of Buddhist concept of non-violence.

Sikhism

Despite being complementary up to a large extent to the

Vedic [Hindu][17] philosophy and accepting valour as its principal value, Sikhism[18] stresses on harmony among human beings and thus calls for mutual cooperation and approval in their day-to-day dealings or activities. Moreover, *Ahimsa* of Sikhism can be observed in its stress on human-unity and fraternity on the one hand, and in its commitment for defending the weak, helpless and women on the other. A Sikh is expected to regard it as his foremost duty, and for its accomplishment, be ready to sacrifice his life. Categorically, non-violence of Sikhism can be viewed in its call and teachings for mutual cooperation, approval and harmony in human transactions, and the certainty of defending others.

Other Eastern Concepts

Besides the above-mentioned four Indian concepts, non-violence can also be discerned in the Confucian doctrine of ***"no return of evil for evil"***[19]; Taoist's emphasis on ***"harmony, humility, yielding to overcome, and seeking to cultivate the feminine side of human nature"*** [20]; Christianity's call for ***"return of hatred by love"***; and Islam's message of ***"fraternity for fraternity"***. All these concepts are imbued with high morality and ethics and thus deeply embedded in non-violence. All of them, having perceptions of human-unity, mutual cooperation, practices and harmony in the centre, call for carrying out daily human practices. In brief, I venture to repeat, these concepts can be viewed integrally connected with high moral values and ethics.

Western Concepts

The Western world, particularly Europe, also is not

immune from concepts pertaining to non-violence. Rather, some of the western concepts are quite ancient and like that of the East, they too are well known and commendable. It is beneficial to mention a few of these. One of those concepts relates to the Greek philosopher Aristotle [384-322 BC]. He, as we know, favoured fostering of attributes. He sought constant development of ethical values of a man so that he could rise to a height.[21] As it is possible only through non-violent tendencies, Aristotle by his advocacy of development of attributes or virtues[22] and ethical values in one way or the other enriched the concept of non-violence. Moreover, he directly or indirectly followed that Greek tradition, which could be linked to great philosophers like Socrates [470/469-399 BC][23] and Plato [428/427-348/347 BC].[24]

For an analysis of the western concept of non-violence, the name of German classical thinker and epistemologist Immanuel Kant [1774-1804] is also worth mentioning. Kant, as known to us, besides being the father of German classical philosophy, was himself a thinker of peace. He stated that it was a practical imperative to treat humanity, whether in your own person or in the person of any other, never simply as a means, but always at the same time as an end.[25]

Supporting the three well-known principles promulgated by Gnaeus Domitius Annius Ulpianus [170-223 AD], anglicized as Ulpian, a Roman Jurisprudent and statesman, that ***"live well as per your natural inclination, never transgress the rights of others, and give their due rights to others"***[26], Immanuel Kant stated that ***be not only the means for others but also an end.***[27]

He laid great stress on non-violation of others' rights on the hand, and for developing relations on the basis of equality on the other; and most particularly on ensuring others' due share. Thus, speaking about equal treatment and good behaviour and especially taking on others' rights, Kant ensured a base to the concept of non-violence; however, his thoughts were focalized on human beings rather than all living beings.

In this same chain the name of English philosopher and reformer Thomas Hill Green [1836-1882] also emerges foremostly. His concept of non-violence is well evident from his statement, particularly made in context of justice. He said, ***"Justice is the habit of mind, which leads us to respect those conditions in dealing with others...not to interfere with them so far as they already exist, and to bring them into existence so far as they are not found in existence."***[28]

Hence, Green presumed non-interference with the existence of living being, and along with this in a positive sense, interference for the promotion of existence and its rise as justice. This justice is undoubtedly complementary to the principle of non-violence, because notions like ***the existence of living being*** **and** ***the promotion of existence*** stimulate the spirit of non-violence.

Other significant Western concepts of non-violence can be found in the views of eminent English Utilitarian thinkers like Jeremy Bentham [1748-1832] and John Stuart Mill [1806-1873]. Non-violence of these thinkers may be observed in their laying stress on realizing one's moral duties towards other human beings on the one hand, and towards animals on the other. They particularly emphasized the moral duty of man towards animals, because they too are sensitive to the feelings of pain and pleasure. Furthermore, an important concept of non-violence prevails in thoughts of the Scottish philosopher Adam Smith [1723-1790],[29] who accepting negative virtue of not hurting one's neighbour as justice, favoured negation of all kinds of violence. This according to Smith, is justice, and undoubtedly symbolic of non-violence.[30]

Moreover, in the views of an Alsatian-German-French theologian and one of the thinkers of the modern age like Albert Schweitzer [1875-1965], who recognized ***"reverence for life as basic principle of ethics"***,[31] also exists a sound concept of non-violence. Schweitzer recognized the ***"right to live as the first right"***[32] and ***"to honour the life as the first duty, not only one's own but also of others"***,[33] as is evident from his own statement in which he said, ***"Ethics grows out of the same root as world and life affirmation, for ethics, too, is nothing but reverence for life. That is what gives me the fundamental principle of morality, namely, that good consists in maintaining, promoting and enhancing life, and that destroying, injuring and limiting life are evil."***[34]

From the above brief survey and analysis of different concepts pertaining to non-violence in the West and the East, particularly India, we reach at the conclusion that despite its being a subject of constant realization and development, as Mahatma Gandhi also admitted[35], *Ahimsa* has been a prime notion not only in the philosophies of religions, but also in the ideas and practices of thinkers and philosophers of repute since ancient times. It has been accepted as the supreme human value since primordial age and at the same time has remained as a dynamic force underlying human activities.

Gandhian Non-Violence

Gandhian concept of *Ahimsa* not only epitomizes a fine coordination among the various concepts of non-violence of India and the rest of Asia, but it also synthesizes different concepts of the East and the West. Furthermore, besides retaining its own exclusive identity, it seems to harmonize among the concepts of non-violence of the ancient, medieval and contemporary periods, and also the modern time. That is why; I have firmly said time and again that Mahatma Gandhi has accorded a wonderful dimension to the theory and practice of *Ahimsa*. After Gautama Buddha it is perhaps only Mahatma Gandhi who effectively and successfully adopted *Ahimsa* according to the demand of time and space in his lifetime. He brought the concept of *Ahimsa* completely out of the domain of extremism, and extended it to enlarge the basis of practices effectively and uniquely in the political sphere. Moreover, he remains the source of inspiration for so many others around the world even after he passed away, particularly for those who desire success through non-violence in socio-political spheres.

It was the success of Gandhi's non-violent measures, which astonished the great scientist Albert Einstein [1879-1955] and made him to conclude, "***Generations to come, it may be, will scarcely believe that such a one as this ever in flesh and blood walked upon this earth.***"[36]

Simultaneously, it encouraged the leader of *African-American Community* of the United States of America Martin Luther King Junior [1929-1968], who had first perceived cowardice in non-violence. But once having examined the Gandhian technique of *Ahimsa*, he reached at the conclusion, even after a decade of Gandhi's passing away, that Gandhi's way was undoubtedly extraordinary, and replete with real potential. He admitted that the Gandhian method of non-violence was one of the sacred and the most potent weapons available to oppressed people in their fight for freedom.[37]

As is evident from Gandhi's statement quoted in the beginning of this text, he accorded a new dimension to the concept of non-violence. There is inherent dynamism in his concept. It has the practicability in its root. Furthermore, it provides for its refinement as per the requirements of time and space.

Along with the above-mentioned statement of the Mahatma, some of his other known statements and writings on the subject apparently reveal harmony and coordination of his concept of *Ahimsa* with the other concepts related to it, and it does not matter if they represent India or other nations of Asia, or the rest of the world. Not only this, they clarify the undisputed relevance and adaptability of Gandhian concept of non-violence in the current perspective.

In one of his articles on non-violence, Mahatma Gandhi wrote, ***"Non-violence is not a rough thing as it has been enunciated. Undoubtedly, it is a part of non-violence to abstain from hurting some living being, but it is only an iota pertaining to its identity. The principle of non-violence is also shattered by every evil thought, false utterance, hatred or wishing something bad unto***

someone. It is also shattered per possession of necessary worldly things."[38]

Similarly, in another article on this subject he pointed out, "***When a person claims to be non-violent, he is expected not be angry with one who has injured him. He will not wish him harm; he will wish him well; he will not swear at him; he will not cause him any physical hurt. He will put up with all the injury to which he is subjected by the wrong-doer. Thus non-violence is complete innocence. Complete non-violence is complete absence of ill-will against all that lives. It therefore embraces sub-human life not excluding noxious insects or beasts...Non-violence is therefore ... active good-will towards all life...***"[39]

After studying and analyzing the above two statements of the Mahatma carefully and minutely, and simultaneously keeping in mind his statement quoted at the outset of this article about non-violence, we arrive at some concrete conclusions. Foremost among them is that the Mahatma undoubtedly represents the general Indian concept of non-violence, which particularly and essentially includes the concepts of *Ahimsa* of *Vedic*-Hinduism, Jainism, Buddhism and Sikhism.[40] In my view it comprises of the following four points:

- The domain of *Ahimsa* [non-violence] encompasses not only human-beings but all living beings;
- In spite of being eternal, natural and the primary human value, *Ahimsa* is a subject of practice as per the demand of time and space;

- *Ahimsa* is an active value; it has nothing to do with cowardice and it is an ornament of the brave; and
- *Ahimsa* is not a subject to be practiced occasionally; in theory and in practice it is all timely.

But, when the Mahatma particularly says that ***"the principle of non-violence is also shattered by every evil thought, false utterance, hate or wishing something bad unto someone"*** and ***"it is a part of non-violence to abstain from hurting some living being, but it is only an iota pertaining to its identity"***, he clearly arrives near the ***Vedic*** concept. At the same time he also appears to relate it to the Jain concept of ***Ahimsa***. This undoubtedly leads to more nearness to Jainism when his views that ***"complete non-violence is complete absence of ill will against that lives"*** and ***"non-violence is therefore ...good will towards all life"*** are examined. But, the Mahatma seems to differ from negative Jain *Ahimsa* when he makes intent behind the act the acid test of violence and non-violence, or when he lays stress on evaluating non-violence on the basis of tendency and pursuance towards spiritual or physical benefit unto everyone.[41]

While writing and speaking about non-violence, the Mahatma has also laid great emphasis on protection, pardon, pity and self-control. In Gandhi's opinion constant development of these virtues is, in fact, the realization of *Ahimsa*. This belief of the Mahatma brings him again nearer to Jainism, Buddhism, and the general Indian concept of non-violence. Further, when he speaks that, ***"the principle of non-violence ...also shattered per possession of necessary worldly things"***, he, along with Indian, arrives near the Asian concepts on the one hand, and to an extent closer to the Western concepts of *Ahimsa* on the other. Moreover, Mahatma Gandhi by combining love and friendliness with non-violence confirms universalism. He also appears to synthesize between East and the West; and old and new concepts of *Ahimsa*.

For Mahatma Gandhi *Ahimsa* is dynamic. It is an active force. Its scope is comprehensive. In his own words:

"Ahimsa is a comprehensive principle. We are helpless mortals caught in the conflagration of himsa. The saying that life lives on life has a deep meaning in it. Man cannot for a moment live without consciously or unconsciously committing outward himsa. The very fact of his living-eating, drinking and moving about-necessarily involves some himsa, destruction of life, be it ever so minute. A votary of Ahimsa therefore remains true to this faith if the spring of all his actions is compassion, if he shuns to the best of his ability the destruction of the tiniest creature, tries to save it, and thus incessantly strives to be free from the deadly coil of himsa. He will be constantly growing in self-restraint and compassion, but he never becomes entirely free from himsa."[42]

Hence, despite bringing harmony among different ideas pertaining to non-violence, Mahatma Gandhi's own related concept seems to be constructive and worth mentioning. Moreover, Gandhi's making the intent behind the act the acid test of *Himsa* or *Ahimsa* and his laying stress on reviewing each and every case relating to violence or non-violence on its own merits independently makes it all the more commendable.

Significance in Current Perspectives

Change is inevitable. Nothing is beyond the law of change. Every sphere of human life is within its range. We ourselves witness change at local, national and international levels. Today's world seems quite different from what it was just twenty-five or fifty years ago. Unprecedented development and constantly growing cooperation among people at all levels and in all walks of life is an effect of the process of this inevitable law of change. Simultaneously, rising competition and self-interests, and resultantly men's indulgence in violent activities is also a consequence of this very process. In fact, it is a natural process. It cannot be denied. Rather, accepting it as a reality, there is the need of making it conducive in larger public interest. In this regard, Gandhian concept pertaining to non-violence can be accepted as an ideal. Particularly in the current perspectives when dangerous clouds loom large around in the sky, and when the whole world seems gripped by many destructive tendencies, Gandhian *Ahimsa* becomes more relevant than even the times of Gandhi. It calls for its refinement and application as per the needs of time and space.

As we have discussed, Gandhian non-violence brings harmony among various concepts pertaining to it [43] on the one hand, and establishes unity in them on the other. Moreover, as per its position[44] it seems to be emerging as an essential condition of existence and human progress. Even, for those, who in a situation contrary to non-violence, take the course of violence and thus indulging in violent activities, connect their acts in one way or the other with the safety of existence and progress, Gandhian *Ahimsa* becomes significant, because it brings common men within its fold. Furthermore, it becomes the subject of practice for all. Concomitantly, it calls for general welfare, mutual acceptance and harmony. Therefore, it clearly seems capable, to a large extent, in controlling dangerous violent tendencies, and transforming the hearts of those involved in violence.

Categorically, for Mahatma Gandhi *Ahimsa* is dynamic; it is truly an active force of the highest order, and indeed soul force.[45] Moreover, it is completely free from any prejudices. Despite its going slow and achieving less than expectations, it has never come in a state of isolation. Rather, its eternal nature is going ahead. Sincerity, acceptance of the situation in current perspective, and readiness to compromise, are among those of its chief features, which are undoubtedly very significant in the global context of the day. And, when these characteristics join the acid test of Gandhian non-violence, its practicability enhances multi-folds. This state of affairs assigns a unique position to Gandhian non-violence and exhorts the people to think over it seriously and adopt it in their day-to-day practices to make human life more prosperous and peaceful.

References:

1. http://answers.google.com/answers/threadview/id/730980.html.

2. http://en.wikipedia.org/wiki/Violence.

3. That is why; a person like Mahatma Gandhi went to the extent of saying, ***"The Rishis, who discovered the law of non-violence in the midst of violence, were greater geniuses than Newton. They were themselves greater warriors than Wellington. Having themselves known the use of arms they realized their uselessness, and taught a weary world that its salvation laid not through violence but through non-violence."*** [Young India, August 11, 1920]

4. *Vedic* [Hinduism or the *Sanatana*], Jainism and Buddhism.

5. Sikhism.

6. Four [the *Rigveda*, the *Yajurveda*, the *Samveda* and the *Atharvaveda*] in number.

7. See the fourth verse of the first *Shloka* of the first *Sukta* of the first *Mandala* of the *Rigveda* [Dayananda *Bhashya* [commentary], in which he explains *Himsa* to be an evil].

8. See the *Yajurveda* 36:18, and the *Atharvaveda* 19:60:1:2 and 19:15:16 respectively.

9. Complete absence of violence is non-violence.

10. Quoted from *Isimasiai Suttai* in Ravindra Kumar's *Non-Violence and Its Philosophy*, page 14

11. This is, at the time of feeling of violence originating against someone, one should see, keeping oneself in one's place. [Theory and Practice of Gandhian Non-Violence, page 7].

12. Desiring mutual cooperation willingly, because this makes the life worth living, prosperous and peaceful. [Ibid]

13. Non-Violence and Its Philosophy, page 14

14. As is evident from the *Dhammapada* [verse 225], meaning thereby, ***"Who practice non-violence and control [their] body, they attain the unchangeable place [Nirvana], and they have***

no reason to suffer thereafter"*, i.e., *"Ahimsaka Ye Munayo Nichcham Kayena Samvuta/ Te Yanti Achchutam Thanam Yattha Gantva Na Sochare//"

15. Which can be observed from the verses [of the *Dhammapada*: 129 and 130] in which Gautama Buddha says, ***"All quiver at punishment, all shudder death; so, considering all equal [to him], a man should not kill [anyone], nor should he has a desire to do so. All are afraid of punishment, and all love life; so, considering all equal [to him], a man should not take life of anyone, nor should he has a desire to do so"*, i.e., *"Sabbe Tasanti Dandassa Sabbe Bhayanti Machchuno/ Attanam Upamam Katva Na Haneyya Na Ghataye// Sabbe Tasanti Dandassa Sabbesam Jivitam Piyam/ Attanam Upamam Katva Na Haneyya Na Ghataye/"***

16. As it is clear from one of the declarations of the Buddha [*Dhammapada*: 270] in which he says, ***"A man is not [an Aryan] noble because he injures living beings; but he is [an Aryan] noble because he is [completely] non-violent and he has pity on all that live"*, i.e., *"Na Ten Ariya Hoti Yen Panani Himsati/ Ahimsa Sabbapananam Ariyo'ti Pavuchchati//"***

17. Or the *Sanatana.*

18. Founded by Guru Nanak Dev [1469-1539 A. D.] during the fifteenth-sixteenth century AD in the Punjab Province.

19. As Confucius himself has said, ***"If a man hurts me, I will return him my affection and good will; the more he hurts me, the kinder I must be; the perfume of goodness reaches me and the sad air of evil blows towards him."*** [Non-Violence and Its Philosophy, page 25].

20. http://www.bsu.edu/libraries/virtualpress/wolfe/word/taoismandnonviolence

21. History of Political Doctrines [Volume-1], page 174

22. This is a character trait or quality valued as being always good in and of itself.

23. In this regard Socrates believed that the best way for people to live was to focus on self-development rather than the pursuit of material wealth and side-by-side his invitation to people to try to concentrate more on friendships and a sense of true community, which according to him was the best way for people to grow together as a populace, is worth mentioning here. [http://en.wikipedia.org/wiki/Socrates].

24. This can be viewed in Plato's theory of justice that is implied to the principles of ***'non-interference'*** and ***'will to fulfill the duties'***, etc.

25. Theory and Practice of Gandhian Non-Violence, page 9

26. History of Political Doctrines [Volume-1], page 259

27. Ibid

28. Theory and Practice of Gandhian Non-Violence, page 10

29. The author of the famous works like *The Theory of Moral Sentiments* and *An Inquiry into the Nature and Causes of the Wealth of Nations*, which is considered by many as the first modern work of economics, and for, Adam Smith is considered as the father of modern economics.

30. Theory and Practice of Gandhian Non-Violence, page 10

31. Ibid, page 11

32. Ibid

33. Ibid

34. Ibid

35. Harijan Sewak, August 11, 1940 [In this regard Mahatma Gandhi has particularly written that all historical evidences

clearly specify that since beginning man has continuously treaded the path of *Ahimsa*. He has also pointed out that if we accept the reality of man's inclination of his going ahead on the pathway to non-violence, it easily proves that he has to go further on the same pathway...].

36. *en.wikiquote.org/wiki/Albert Einstein.*

37. *See Non-Cooperation* by the same author.

38. Theory and Practice of Gandhian Non-Violence, page 25 [Originally q*uoted from Mangal Prabhat* 1945]

39. Young India, March 2, 1922

40. See India and Mahatma Gandhi by the same author.

41. Theory and Practice of Gandhian Non-Violence, page 25

42. Ibid, page 26

43. It doesn't matter if they are from the East or the West, or if they represent the ancient or medieval periods, or the modern age.

44. Being the supreme human value.

45. In this regard the Mahatma wrote, ***"It is soul force or the power of Godhead within us. Imperfect man cannot grasp the whole of the Essence- he would not be able to bear its full blaze, but even an infinitesimal fraction of it, when it becomes active within us, can work wonders."***

Bibliography:

- Gandhi, MK [ed.]. 1940. *Harijan Sewak Weekly.* Ahmedabad [India]: Harijan Sewak Sangh and Navajivan Trust.
- Gandhi, MK [ed.]. 1919-31. *Young India Weekly*. [Reprinted in 13 Volumes in 1984]. Ahmedabad [India]: Navajivan Publishing House.

- Gratsiyanski, PS, Grafaski, VG, Deyev, NN, Nersesyants, VS and Mamut, LS. 1976-80. *History of Political Doctrines* [Four Volumes in Hindi]. Moscow: Progress Publication.
- Kumar, Ravindra. 2007. *Gautama Buddha and the Dhammapada*. New Delhi [India]: Kalpaz Publications.
- Kumar, Ravindra. 2010. *India and Mahatma Gandhi*. New Delhi [India]: Kalpaz Publications.
- Kumar, Ravindra. 2009. *Non-Cooperation*. Meerut [India]: World Peace Movement Trust.
- Kumar, Ravindra. 2003. *Non-Violence and Its Philosophy*. Meerut [India]: Dynamic Publications.
- Kumar, Ravindra. 2002. *Theory and Practice of Gandhian Non-Violence*. New Delhi [India]: Mittal Publications.
- Shastri, Manohar Muni. 1963. *Isimasiai Suttai*. Mumbai [India]: MNS

*****

2

Global Peace Movement and Relevance of Gandhian View

"I will not sacrifice Truth and Ahimsa even for the deliverance of my country or religion" **–MK Gandhi**

"Mahatma Gandhi embodied in his life certain universal principles that are inherent in the moral structure of the universe, and these principles are as inescapable as the law of gravitation." –Martin Luther King Junior

Martin Luther King Junior in his above-mentioned statement clearly emphasizes the following about Mahatma Gandhi:

One, Gandhi's life was brimming with certain universal principles or values; secondly, the impossibility to escape from the reality of universal principles or values. In other words, acceptance of these important universal principles or values cannot be denied.

King Junior also highlighted that there is a moral structure for the human world and universal values identify the human world, and they are the conditions of a civilized life.

In this regard my own view is that morality itself is one of the three[1] fundamentals of civilization. I have explained this in length in my book entitled, *The Fundamentals of Civilization*. But, without deviating from the topic in hand it suffices to say that without morality there is no possibility of a civilized life. In the absence of morality, civilization is completely meaningless. Finally, morality is the true ornament of human life and as Mahatma Gandhi himself pointed out, it helps ***"in finding out the true path for us and in fearlessly following it."***[2]

Further, placing the Mahatma in the centre of the statement by King, we may arrive at the conclusion that morality, one of the chief universal values that conditions civilized life, was among those universal principles that characterized Gandhi's life.

And, it is true. Gandhi's life was imbued with morality. It was the basis of his ideas, activities and works. He stressed on this aspect urging humanity to adopt it ***"consciously and as a matter of duty."***[3] More particularly, the supreme human value *Ahimsa* [non-violence], of which morality itself is one of the supplementary values or one which absolutely stays within its domain, was the nucleus in the life and works of the Mahatma. In this context the words of Mahatma Gandhi that, ***"I will not sacrifice Truth and Ahimsa even for the deliverance of my country or religion"***[4], are sufficient to exemplify this fact.

Ahimsa, an essential condition of existence, development and achievement of the life's goal, was the core of all of Gandhi's activities. Perhaps for the first time in the entire human history Mahatma Gandhi applied non-violence in its refined form and as per the demand of time and space in the political sphere; he adopted *Ahimsa* as a means to achieve unprecedented success. He established with certainty that on the strength of non-violence, evils like exploitation, inequality and slavery could be eliminated. All kinds of estrangements, disputes, conflicts, hostilities and struggles could be settled amicably whereby conflict and disagreement could be transformed into a state of harmony and peace. That is why; a great man like Martin Luther King Junior spoke about the Mahatma the way he did.

Gandhism [amalgamation of *Ahimsa*-based ideas and practices of Mahatma Gandhi] essentially and inevitably became in one way or the other, the centre of every movement launched by him and his colleagues for achieving equality and freedom. Many others like Martin Luther King Junior followed *Ahimsa* with the purpose of establishing peace and justice.

II

My emphasis on the subject could easily bring up the question why Gandhism is necessary today. To deliver a satisfactory answer I think it would be appropriate to discuss first why we need to launch movements for peace? More particularly, why peace-movements are necessary internationally in these days when the world is fast converting into a global village?

In fact, peace is an active and dynamic state in which one gets the opportunity to move forward towards development without confusion, fear or worry. On the other hand conflicts, disputes, dissensions, fights or struggles are illustrative of the absence of peace. Undoubtedly, harmony, cooperation and love emerge as chief characteristics of the state of peace. Despite several negative human tendencies, efforts for progress are desired by all since advancement at all levels and in all walks of life is a prime necessity of human life. In other words, it is a part and parcel of human endeavours. Hence, through the ages man has made constant efforts to gain peace either by individual or by collective means. This state remains intact today and will be so in the times to come.

Before proceeding further one more thing should be

clarified. Peace is a dynamic state and not a situation of the status quo. Furthermore, it has nothing to do with inactiveness. In a state of peace, man accepting the reality of *Vasudhaiv Kutumbakam*[5], and freeing himself from the state of confusion, fear, tension, conflict, struggle and war, through harmony and cooperation of others in society continuously work to ensure welfare of humanity. Peace is also the best means to progress.[6] Hence, it can be asserted that through the ages efforts for peace have been made individually or collectively and for this the method of non-cooperation has also been adopted from time-to-time.[7] Today, because of the unprecedented scale of globalization, the importance and the need for such an effort multiplies many folds, more than in the past.

Now, let us talk about the subject in hand, i.e., peace and Gandhian view, in particular the adaptability, importance and significance of Gandhian view and vision of the establishment of peace globally!

As we know, the Gandhian view in general pertains to the welfare of the human world. Moreover, Mahatma Gandhi carried out his practices accordingly. Whatever he preached he practiced them to clearly illustrate to the world that his life itself was his message. Therefore, it is necessary to take his ideas and practices together while discussing or analyzing his views. We can categorically say that Gandhian approach or view can be comprehended in real sense only if his ideas and practices are both put together in perspective.

Firstly, the basis or the centre of Gandhian view

is *Ahimsa* [non-violence] as the highest human value. *Ahimsa* is a natural and eternal value. Besides being the essential condition for the existence *Ahimsa* is the means of development and achieving the goal of life. All high human values, including morality, at the centre of this discussion, originate from *Ahimsa*. Furthermore, *Ahimsa* itself is also the protector of all human values and the basis of ethics. Therefore, thousands of years ago, *Ahimsa* was declared as the *Parmodharma*[8] by the *Vedic*-Hindu philosophy and it was also accepted as the *Parmabrahaman*[9] by Jainism.

Hence, *Ahimsa* is interpreted as the basis of the supreme moral law. It is the foundation of universal principles and also its leading force. It is an eternal law or the rule. To repeat, *Ahimsa* is the essential condition for existence and continuity. This fact is emphasized by Martin Luther King Junior who underlined the non-violent philosophy of the Mahatma many a time. For example he said, ***"I found in the non-violent resistance philosophy of Gandhi... the only morally and practically sound method open to oppressed people in their struggle for freedom."***[10]

Secondly, Gandhian view admits the reality of differences, disputes, conflicts and struggles, and their impact on various walks of human life.[11] It accepts cooperation and struggle both as the necessities of society.[12] But, at the same time it is determined to settle or resolve all states of violence by adopting *Ahimsa* in its refined form as per the demand of time and space. Thus, admitting the reality of the law of change Gandhism calls for resolution and solution of each and every struggle and dispute through the value of *Ahimsa*. In comparison to other available methods of conflict resolution Gandhism has a certain distinct and striking sense of justice. That is why; for almost a century the people of the world have looked at this method with high hopes and expectations. Not only this, some of the non-violent actions launched per the Gandhian way in different parts of the world achieved unprecedented successes. The actions launched by Afro-Americans under the leadership of Martin Luther King Junior himself in the United States of America could be well counted in this very perspective.

The attraction and curiosity of people all over the world towards the distinctive Gandhian view seems to increase day-by-day to revitalize high hopes in the hearts of people more than in the past. With on-going globalization, the genesis of new problems, disputes and conflicts seems inevitable. That is why; the Gandhian view in resolving these problems emerges as one of the best and noble alternatives available to the world. It can show the people the pathway to prosperity and peace opening the doors to both prosperity and peace through mass awakening, cooperation and participation of people. This is the uniqueness of the Gandhian view. For, Martin Luther King Junior [quoting him again] went to the extent of observing the personality of the Mahatma in the sixth decade of the last century:

"Gandhi was probably the first person in history to lift the love ethic of Jesus above mere interaction between individuals to a powerful and effective social force..."[13]

III

In the current perspective, when globalization is on rise day-by-day, Gandhian view fully imbued by *Ahimsa*, has special significance for those working for peace at the global level. It is because Gandhian view accepts all the spheres of human life as the essential parts of an ***'Indivisible Whole'***. To quote the Mahatma himself, ***"You cannot divide life, social, economic, political and purely religious, into watertight compartments."***[14]

Furthermore, Gandhi accepted the reality of interconnectedness of all spheres of life and discussed their essential and inevitable effect on one-another and, therefore, called for solution of conflicts, disputes, problems and struggles without any prejudice. He particularly inspired and encouraged the people to be ready to action to win justice, freedom and equality on the basis of high human values, particularly *Ahimsa*. He called for readiness to compromise always, but without surrendering self-respect, and by abiding to truth and morality.

This reality could be well testified particularly in the two local-regional level *Satyagrahas* namely Champaran[15] and Kheda[16] [1917-8], which were carried out under the leadership of Gandhi himself and in Nagpur[17] Flag *Satyagraha* [1923], Borsad[18] *Satyagraha* [1924] the Bardoli[19] Peasants' Struggle [1928], fought under the leadership of Vallabhbhai Patel, the Rajkot[20] *Satyagraha* [1938-39], initiated under the leadership of both the Mahatma and the Sardar, Vaikom[21] *Satyagraha* [1924-25], initiated under the leadership of TK Madhavan[22], and at national level Civil Disobedience

Movement [1930][23] launched by Gandhi by breaking the Salt Law.[24] All of them were more or less successful. However, the Bardoli Peasants' Struggle was unique and unprecedented as it created history. All of them greatly inspired the people, not only Indians, but so many others in the world. They set a clear direction for non-violent struggles [*Satyagrahas*] to be launched in times to come in different parts of the world. Although an account of the series of events pertaining to these is available in the history books, there is still a need for their fair and comprehensive analysis.

Along with this, a comprehensive and critical analysis of Afro-American struggles, particularly the ones that commenced in the sixth and seventh decades of the Twentieth Century, [25] in particular the initiatives of Martin Luther King Junior that acquainted the present generation of the impact of Gandhian view is also required. As we all know King accepted and adopted Gandhian way in the Afro-American struggles as he saw fit, the best means among all the ways and methods available for depressed classes in their fight for equality and freedom in his own land. By doing so, the relevance and aptness of Gandhian view in the peace movements at national and global levels would become apparent to us to step forward on the pathway to peace in the Twenty-First Century.

References:

1. The other two fundamentals are: *Ahimsa* [non-violence] and freedom.

2. Defining morality and connecting it with righteousness also, the Mahatma has pointed out, ***"Morality is to attain mastery***

over our mind and our passions." [See MK Gandhi's *Hind Swarajya*, Chapter XIII].

3. *Epic Fast*, page 43

4. *Young India*, January 20, 1927 (This small statement is a par tof Mahatma Gandhi's reply to a critic who wrote him in context of his article in tribute to Swami Shradhanand. The full text of Gandhi's reply has been placed in Appendix-1)

5. *Vasudhaiv Kutumbakam* denotes to ancient *Vedic*-Hindu concept of human-unity. It means the entire earth is but one family.

6. Including certainty of existence.

7. See Non-Cooperation by the same author.

8. Religion in grandeur.

9. It denotes to the Supreme Authority.

10. http://stream.state.gov/streamvol/libmedia/india/13974/mlkradioaudio/mlkonair1959.mp3 [All India Broadcast, March 9, 1959].

11. Which could be realized from his write up in the issue of *Harijan* of October 26, 1947 in which he had admitted, ***"How could the fact be undone?"***

12. Ibid

13. http://nobelprize.org/nobel_prizes/peace/laureates/1964/press.html

14. Gandhian Thought: New World, New Dimensions [In this regard the Mahatma further went to the extent of saying, ***"I do not know any religion apart from human activity. It provides a moral basis of all other activities, which they would otherwise lack, reducing life to a maze of sound and fury signifying nothing."***].

15. In Bihar.

16. Presently in Gujarat.

17. Presently in Maharashtra.

18. In Gujarat.

19. Ibid

20. Ibid

21. TK Madhavan [1885-1930], a leading and popular Indian social reformer from Kerala, who led the struggle at Vaikom during 1924-5 against untouchability in orthodox Hindu society. This struggle is known as Vaikom *Satyagraha.*

22. Vaikom *Satyagraha* was a historical agitation in Travancore, one of the Indian Princely States, [presently a part of Kerala Province]. The movement was centred at the Shiva Temple at Vaikom, near Kottayam and the chief aim of the *Satyagraha* remained at securing freedom of movement for all sections of society through the public roads leading to the Sri Mahadevar Temple of Vaikom.

23. The Civil Disobedience Movement besides being the second nationwide struggle of Indians for the freedom under the leadership of Mahatma Gandhi was also unique as people at large scale participated in it.

24. At Dandi [in Gujarat], which began on March 12, 1930 from the *Sabarmati Ashram* of Gandhi in Ahmedabad and concluded on April 6, 1930 with the breaking of the Salt Law by the Mahatma.

25. Especially, the Montgomery Bus Boycott [1955], the Albany Movement [1961], the Birmingham Campaign [1963], and the March of Washington [1963].

Bibliography:

- Bhave, Vinoba. 1973. *Vinoba on Gandhi.* Wardha [India]: Sarva Sewa Sangh.
- Carter, Candice and Kumar, Ravindra. 2010. *Peace Philosophy in Action.* New York [USA]: Palgrave Macmillan.
- Gandhi, MK. 1927. *An Autobiography or the Story of My Experiments with Truth.* Ahmedabad [India]: Navajivan Publishing House.
- Gandhi, MK. [ed.]. 1919-31. *Young India Weekly.* [Reprinted in 13 Volumes in 1984]. Ahmedabad [India]: Navajivan Publishing House.
- Kumar, Ravindra. 2006. *Fundamentals of Civilization* [in Hindi]. New Delhi [India]: Gyan Publishing House.
- Kumar, Ravindra. 2008. *Gandhian Thought: New World, New Dimensions.* Delhi [India]: Kalpaz Publications.
- Kumar, Ravindra. 2009. *Non-Cooperation.* Meerut [India]: World Peace Movement Trust.

*****

3

A Civil Society of Gandhi's Imagination

"[Those] who accept the ideal of attaining self-control as the highest duty of man, and are fired by a genuine and undying faith in their mission, and are sleeplessly vigilant and active, their labour will light the path..."

–MK Gandhi

"If national life becomes so perfect as to become self-regulated, no representation becomes necessary. There is then a state of enlightened anarchy. In such a state, everyone is his own ruler. He rules himself in such a manner that he is never a hindrance to his neighbour."

–MK Gandhi

Just in the above short statement of the Mahatma, we could more or less perceive a civil society of his imagination. In other words, we could draw an outline of the civil society of his dreams. How? Before comprehending and realizing it, and that too along with its significance in the current perspectives, it is contextual if we become familiar with the word meaning and general concept of civil society.

There are two words in civil society: civil and society. Here civil in fact connotes to civilized, which again is an adjective of the word civil. Civil undoubtedly relates to the human being, a civic. Moreover, along with civic, referring to his place, the city, it specifies characteristics, works and programmes of both of them. Similarly, the word civilized reveals high qualities of man, the civic, evolutionary culture, behaviour and work. Particularly, features like good conduct, control, organization, and the wish for peace are within its ambit. They are essentially included in it. System, cooperation and continuous steps towards development are its foremost signs.

Human society, with which only the word civilized can be associated, is generally a group of people related to each other through persistent relations; people share the same geographical territory under one authority and within the ambit of one culture in general, more or less, carried out their day-to-day practices. They step forward for the safety of existence and progress.

If we define society from the word meaning viewpoint, it is in fact derived of the Latin word *Societas*; that again is the creation of *Socius*, a noun of the same Latin, which describes unity of the people, organization and the process of their harmony. Hence, society is an organization, which connects those who come within its ambit culturally. It accords unity to them and make them co-sharers of all the gains.

In short, a civil society is the revelation of social structure of men, which is full of high values, human characteristics and practices.

II

After becoming familiar with word meaning and concept of civil, civilized and society, now it is appropriate to examine the statement of the Mahatma, which has been quoted in the beginning of the discussion at hand.

From the above-mentioned statement of Mahatma Gandhi, the following four points emerge categorically:

1. Perfect national life;
2. State of enlightenment;
3. Self-rule [self-control and discipline]; and
4. No hindrance to neighbour [Harmony and cooperation with others]

A civil society of the imagination of the Mahatma could be well perceived in these four points existing in his statement. These points may seem us hypothetical, moral and simple, but in reality they are full of high human values and the acid test of a civilized life. As much, these points are made the subject of human behaviour as the true development of society is feasible; success for the establishment of a civil society of the imagination of Mahatma Gandhi is possible. Let us now discuss these points one-by-one!

Perfect National Life

A perfect national life of the perception of Gandhi, although cannot astray of *Ahimsa* [non-violence][1] with morality and ethics in public affairs as its foremost features, but the Mahatma especially and essentially desired respect of freedom of each and every one in such a national life. In other words, he stressed on freedom in equal proportion for one and all. In his own words, ***"...Weakest should have [along with freedom] the same opportunity as the strongest."***[2]

On the basis of this, Mahatma Gandhi visualized a national life. More or less it was the reflection of his concept of *Swarajya*, stepping towards the establishment of the *Ramarajya*.

State of Enlightenment

The second feature of civil society of Gandhi's imagination could be observed in his stress on the state of enlightenment. In it, one and all individuals, society and nation are expected to be fully conscious of their respective duties. In place of asking for rights, to know and perform duties are in fact the basis of a true state of enlightenment. With the performance of duties, one attains rights naturally. In the words of the Mahatma himself, ***"Rights accrue automatically to him who duly performs his duties.*** **[Not only this],** ***in fact, the right to perform one's duties is the only right that is worth living for and dying for. It covers all legitimate rights."***[3]

It is the duty, if performed well, which along with making individuals conscious, lead them to the true pathway to all-round development. For this, it is necessary that all, individuals, communities, societies and nations, well perform their respective duties. Therefore, Gandhi laid the stress on it. Categorically, enlightenment by performing duties and by enlightenment the rise and welfare of all [*Sarvodaya*] was, for him, a concrete means of *Swarajya*, therefore, the *Ramarajya*.

Self-Rule [Self-Control and Discipline]

Self-control by discipline is the acid test of a true human being that paves the way to self-rule in the best manner. It is the state opposite to such liberty, which burdened some others. Rather, it must continuously develop humanity on the one hand, and should make freedom meaningful on the other.[4] Moreover, it should accord strength to the rule of the people[5] and develop the spirit of sacrifice in one and all.

Mahatma Gandhi was of the firm opinion that discipline develops the spirit of sacrifice in man and where discipline and sacrifice both exist, people while fighting non-violently against injustice and oppression, march forward towards the establishment of a civil society.[6]

Thus, self-control by self-discipline plays an important role in preparing concrete ground for self-rule, which is necessary for true human development, worldly and spiritually, in other words, for a civil society of the imagination of the Mahatma. Moreover, Gandhi considered it to be the foremost duty. To quote him, **"[Those]** ***who accept the ideal of attaining self-control as the highest duty of man, and are fired by a genuine and undying faith in their mission, and are sleeplessly vigilant and active, their labour will light the path..."***[7]

No Hindrance to Neighbour [Harmony and Cooperation with Others]

The fourth feature of civil society of Gandhi's imagination, particularly having the statement of the Mahatma, quoted at the commencement of this discussion, as the nucleus, could be observed in his own words '*never a hindrance to his neighbour*', which means not to interfere in others' affairs while carrying out day-to-day practices. In these words remains the spirit of '*Live and Let Live*', which is symbolic of tolerance and forbearance. Further, certainty of others' freedom and fraternity also seem to be there. With cooperation and coordination of people, there is a call to step forward for large scale welfare at individual, community, society and national levels.

Especially, tolerance and forbearance always escalates the spirit of cooperation and coordination in men. They, by transforming conflicts and resolving disputes[8], pave the way for peace. In the state of peace, people after becoming free from confusion, fear, terror and violence, march forward continuously for welfaristic causes with courage and zeal. Hence, they strengthen human values and contribute in getting society more and more civilized.

Thus, the above four points from Gandhi's own statement, to a large extent, clarifies the imagination of the Mahatma about a civil society. All the four points — perfect national life, state of enlightenment, self-rule and no hindrance to neighbor — in fact, instead of being important for a civil society of the imagination of Gandhi, are equally essential and inevitable for any of the civil societies. These points are filled with morality that itself is one of the fundamentals of civilization[9], ethics and equality in opportunities, and simultaneously, they ascertain freedom to one and all. Further, in them there is a call for duty, consciousness, self-control and sacrifice in the larger welfare of humanity. High human values along with the expectation of '*Live and Let Live*' emerge in them. The role of any of these in the making of civility cannot be denied or underestimated. Therefore, the Gandhian vision of a civil society can also not be undervalued.

Critical Analysis

All those who are familiar with Gandhian philosophy, know that it is fully within the ambit of *Ahimsa*. Not a single aspect of his views is untouched by non-violence and its complementary values including morality. How then a civil society of his imagination can be unaffected by it? For this reason many in the world, while commenting on Gandhian views, try to declare them to be just hypothetical. They talk of their being the part of ethics and moral studies, which have been taught by others also from time-to-time. They question of a further ideal in them.

In reply to these kinds of suspicions, it could be asserted with certainty that despite making *Ahimsa* and other values complimentary to it the basis of his views, the Mahatma never asked to bring any viewpoint within the domain of perpetuity. He called for bringing every human value, including *Ahimsa*, a subject of refinement so that it could prove to be all- welfaristic in prevailing circumstances of space. Many of his *Ahimsa*-based actions well prove this fact and they are simultaneously capable of removing all such suspicions. Further, they are capable of proving significance of Gandhi's ideas in the current perspectives.

Mahatma Gandhi categorically called for not to adhere to any view or philosophy just for the reason that it had been the most effective on a certain point of history. He declared any of the blind following to be foolishness. Refinement in ideas as per the demand of time and space is necessary; their conduciveness and practicability in a prevailing situation is inevitable for the larger welfare of humanity. Hence, it is enough to prove the relevance of Gandhian views. There is a need to make fair examination of Gandhi's ideas pertaining to a civil society of his imagination and along with this, to work in this direction.

References:

1. He, particularly having the concept of democracy in the centre put forth in Harijan on November 11, 1938, ***"If they [states] are to become true [to work in the largest interest of people and***

perfect] for equal welfare of all, they must become courageously non-violent."

2. Harijan, May 18, 1940

3. Ibid, May 27, 1939

4. In this regard Mahatma Gandhi went to the extent of saying in Young India on June 3, 1926, ***"The highest form of freedom carries with it the greatest measure of discipline and humility. Freedom that comes from discipline and humility cannot be denied, unbridled licence is a sign of vulgarity injurious alike to self and one's neighbours."***

5. For, he had put forth in Young India on July 7, 1930, ***"Democracy [government of the people] disciplined and enlightened is the finest thing..."*** And, as written by him in Harijan also on May 27, 1939, ***"A democrat is a born disciplinarian..."***

6. See India of My Dreams by Gandhi, MK.

7. Harijan, November 21, 1936

8. Admitting the importance of tolerance Gandhi wrote in Young India on July 30, 1931 that without tolerance we would unable to settle our differences, disputes or conflicts.

9. The other two are: non-violence and freedom.

Bibliography:

- Gandhi, MK. 1927. *An Autobiography or the Story of My Experiments with Truth*. Ahmedabad [India]: Navajivan Publishing House.
- Gandhi, MK [ed.]. 1933-41, 1942-8. *Harijan Weekly*. Ahmedabad [India]: Harijan Sewak Sangh and Navajivan Trust.

- Gandhi, MK. 1947. *India of My Dreams*. Ahmedabad [India]: Navajivan Publishing House.
- Gandhi, MK [ed.]. 1919-31. *Young India Weekly*. [Reprinted in 13 Volumes in 1984]. Ahmedabad [India]: Navajivan Publishing House.
- Kumar, Ravindra. 2001. *Gandhi and Gandhism* [Part-1]. Meerut [India]: World Peace Movement Trust.
- Kumar, Ravindra. 2006. *Fundamentals of Civilization* [in Hindi]. New Delhi [India]: Gyan Publishing House.

*****

4

Gandhian View of Civilization

"If Swarajya was not mean to civilize us, and to purify and stabilize our civilization, it would be nothing worth. The very essence of our civilization is that we give a paramount place to morality in all our affairs, public or private."

–MK Gandhi

Introduction

Civilization, which is *Sabhyata* in Indian term, is derived from the word *Civil*, *Sabhya*. From its word meaning viewpoint, it generally denotes the skillfulness in practice. Undoubtedly, when this word is associated with man, it identifies his characteristics. As culture introduces attributes or qualities [*Samskaras*] of an individual, a group of individuals, community, society or nation, approximately in the same manner through civilization evolutionary characteristics of people of a particular region or a country are known. In other words, practices and development of people is observed.

Evolution

Civilization is a subject of continuous development and this development, as Radhakrishnan describes, is a matter of mind. [Kumar, *Fundamentals of Civilization*, page 17/ *Radhakrishnan, Speeches and Writings*, May 1962-May 1964, page 430].

With a firm and constructive approach, stepping forward on the pathway to advancement at all levels and in all walks of life is an essential condition of making a civilization. A state contrary to it can emphatically be the ground of fall of a civilization. The pages of the whole available history verify this fact.

So many civilizations developed in different parts of the world from time-to-time. Some of them touched such heights that even their remains, and particularly ruined structures fill us with great surprises today. They force us to rethink about their unique system and techniques used in those days, when despite the lack of development in the field of science and technology and limited available resources in which making arrangement was not an easy task, they added dimensions one after the other to the pathway to progress. They urge us to study and analyze fundaments of thousand years' old civilizations of Egypt, Mesopotamia, Greece, China, Babylonia and India.

For years, archeologists and historians have been studying and analyzing all of these civilizations. They have been adopting different methods for the purpose. But, still they have not arrived at any unanimous conclusion in this regard. Despite all this, one thing is quite clear, and that is for the making of civilization development is necessary, and for development a high mentality is essential. I repeat that this is the only truth about those civilizations, which developed in various parts of the world from time-to-time. Moreover, the fall of various civilizations could also be analyzed having the above arguments in the centre.

For the development and stability of a civilization it is necessary that it should be free from the state of isolation. Furthermore, it goes forward on the basis of coordination with others as per the demand of time. Despite numerous differences, it adopts liberal attitude and accepts and assimilates whatever is good in others. In this regard, the following statement of Mahatma Gandhi is worth mentioning:

"This is not to say that we may not adopt and assimilate whatever may be good and capable of assimilation by us..." [1]

Gandhian View

Mahatma Gandhi seems fully in consonance with all the three chief fundamentals of civilization-*Ahimsa* [non-violence], morality and freedom while he talks, discusses and ventures to analyze it. In other words, he himself seems committed to develop civilization having these three in the centre. Moreover, everybody knows Gandhi's commitment to *Ahimsa*. Despite this, his following short statements in context of non-violence, which besides being an eternal and natural human value, is also the first and essential fundamental of civilization, make everything clear in this regard:

"Man has made constant development toward Ahimsa."[2]

And,

"For progress, humanity paced forward towards non-violence."[3]

Mahatma Gandhi was determined to make *Ahimsa* conducive in prevailing situations and on the basis of it to step forward on pathway to development. This was the way of making and stabilizing civilization. In this regard particularly in Indian context he said:

"I believe absolutely that India has a mission for all in the world. She is not to copy...blindly, but showing way of peace and progress on the strength of Ahimsa."[4]

Not only this, in context of a new building of *Swarajya* in India, or in other words in context of the remaking of a refined and evolutionary civilization, he also clarified:

"In my Swarajya basic genesis of civilization will remain intact. I will write many new things for India, but on my own slate [in its own circumstances and on the basis of its traditions and values]." [5]

His indication is clear. He is all for *Ahimsa*, which has from ancient times been an accepted *Dharma* in India. Moreover, it is the means of security of existence and development.

Morality is the second fundamental of civilization. Like *Ahimsa* morality was also important for Mahatma Gandhi, which is evident from his commitment to it. In this regard his following statement is worth quoting:

"If Swarajya was not mean to civilize us, and to purify and stabilize our civilization, it would be nothing worth. The very essence of our civilization is that we give a paramount place to morality in all our affairs, public or private." [6]

In fact, superior human virtues are discovered through morality. That is why; morality is a value dedicated to one's duty and to the welfare of all. Simultaneously, it is an essential condition of humankind; therefore, one of the chief fundamentals of civilization. In the *Vedic*-Hindu philosophy and the way of life it is an indispensable part of duties to be performed by its followers. Along with this, wellbeing of civilization is possible by keeping it intact in day-to-day human practices. Hence, it has been said that if morality is accepted as a supreme law of being, ***"all other laws will get clear automatically."*** [7]

Freedom is the third among the chief fundaments of civilization. It is an important condition of life not only for human beings but all living beings. Although, through the ages different opinions or views have been put forth by thinkers or philosophers about it; Hobbes, Locke, Rousseau, Marx and many others have defined it from their own respective viewpoint, but undoubtedly freedom, in its real meaning, completes when the one assures others' freedom at the time of enjoying it for self. Enjoying freedom on the cost of others is of no worth; it is not fruitful. If someone does so, ***"he goes against the basic spirit of freedom."***[8]

How much Mahatma Gandhi was concerned of freedom, whole world knows. The whole Gandhian philosophy and actions of the Mahatma well prove his sincerity, longing and commitment to freedom. In this regard his following statement is worth mentioning here:

"If individual freedom goes, then surely all is lost; for, if the individual ceases to count, what is left of society? Individual freedom also can make a man voluntarily surrender himself completely to the service of society. If it is wrested from him, he becomes automation and society is ruined. No society can possibly be built on denial of individual freedom."[9]

Thus, freedom is necessary for growth or development. Freedom with equality is inevitable for each and everyone for the making of a true civilization and its stabilization. Therefore, accepting all the three chief fundamentals of civilization as the nucleus, Gandhi steps forward in this regard and draws the attention of the world in general and India in particular to the following three points:

- Civilization is a subject of conformity according to time and space;
- Civilization is not a subject of imitating others; blind following in the name of civilization never brings fruits; and
- In the making and developing of civilization only that should be accepted from others, which contributes in strengthening indigenous civilization and simultaneously, which suits in prevailing circumstances, and helps in coordination with basic indigenous elements.

Undoubtedly, Gandhi's views in the making, developing and strengthening civilization seem important. Furthermore, the relevance of these ideas of Gandhi for the whole world in general, and especially for a country of diversity like India becomes more important today when India is ready to play the vital role in the world affairs and the whole world is looking towards India.

References:

1. Young India, April 30, 1931
2. Harijan Sewak, August 11, 1941
3. Gandhi's Challenge to Communism, page 23
4. See India of My Dreams.
5. Ibid

6. Young India, January 23, 1930
7. Fundamentals of Civilization, page 38
8. Ibid, page 47
9. Gandhi and Gandhism, page 19

Bibliography:

- Gandhi, MK [ed.]. 1933-41, 1942-8. *Harijan Weekly.* Ahmedabad [India]: Harijan Sewak Sangh and Navajivan Trust.
- Gandhi, MK [ed.]. 1933-41, 1942-8. *Harijan Sewak Weekly.* Ahmedabad [India]: Harijan Sewak Sangh and Navajivan Trust.
- Gandhi, MK. 1957. *India of My Dreams.* Ahmedabad [India]: Navajivan Publishing House.
- Gandhi, MK [ed.]. 1919-31. *Young India Weekly.* [Reprinted in 13 Volumes in 1984]. Ahmedabad [India]: Navajivan Publishing House.
- Kripalani, JB. 1970. *Gandhi: His Life and Thought.* New Delhi [India]: Publications Division of Ministry of Information and Broadcasting, Government of India.
- Kumar, Ravindra. 2006. *Fundamentals of Civilization* [in Hindi]. New Delhi [India]: Gyan Publishing House.
- Kumar, Ravindra. 2001. *Gandhi and Gandhism* [Part-1]. Meerut [India]: World Peace Movement Trust.
- Kumar, Ravindra. 2006. *Religion and World Peace.* New Delhi [India]: Gyan Publishing House.

*****

5
Education and Peace : With Reference to Gandhian Viewpoint

"Education can help mould and shape the human body, mind and character in such a manner that they may act as the means to achieve joy and efficiency."

–MK Gandhi

"By education I mean an all-round drawing out of the best in child and man-body, mind and spirit. Literacy is not the end of education or even the beginning."

–MK Gandhi

Education certainly is a means to all-round progress of man. In other words, the pathway to human-development goes through the lanes of education. Moreover, true education is the sole basis of achieving one's purpose in life. It is education, which can ascertain ultimate peace for a human being.

Needless to say, the importance of education in man's life cannot be described in words. In addition, the essence of all the ancient scriptures, messages of scholars and thinkers of repute have always categorically expounded the significance of education in human life. By illustrating the mutual relationship between the education and peace, they have also declared education as the means and basis of peace. Furthermore, they enlighten people of the importance of education in all walks of life, in particular, its role in making life prosperous and peaceful under the prevailing circumstances. Further, the implications in the absence of true education, especially in creating an atmosphere of disharmony and conflict are examined. In this regard the following *Shloka* from an oldest Hindu scripture is worth quoting here:

"माता शत्रु पिता वैरी येन बालो न पाठितः
न शोभते सभा मध्ये हंस मध्ये वाको यथा।"

"Mata Shatru Pita Vairi Yen Balo Na Pathitah, Na Shobhate Sabha Madhye Hans Madhye Vako Yatha"

Meaning thereby: The parent who does not facilitate and guide the child for studies is like the greatest enemy of the child. The presence of an uneducated person in the company of educated people is like a goose in the company of swans.

The utility, significance and importance of education are inevitable at all levels in all walks of life. It develops into the most beautiful and valuable ornament of human life.

Now, before further discussion regarding mutual relations between education and peace, we should understand the meaning and purpose of the both-education and peace-separately. To do so with particularly emphasis on the Gandhian view is important and considered the prudent approach for this article.

Education

The English meaning for education is derived from the Latin word *Educare*, which further relates to *Educere*, the symbolic of manifestation or expression. This definition reveals the inner capability of man that guides him continuously at various levels. The whole process, which leaves an impact upon the mind, character and physical strength, plays a vital role in human development. It accords continuity to intellect, knowledge and values, which provides the base and scope of education.

If we analyze education from the Indian viewpoint, education [*Shiksha*] is one of the six *Vedangas*.[1] Clarity of understanding and systematic method or the orders, which are the basics for the all-round development of one's personality, are within its domain. Hence, the educational process is fully dedicated to continuity; it is for growth or for accumulation; it is the means to lead a human being on the pathway to prosperity in prevailing circumstances on the basis of knowledge and accomplishments.

Peace

The use of popular English word *peace* can be found in words like *Pax* [Vulgate], *Eirene* [Greek] and *Shalom* [Hebrew]. Besides desiring harmony in day-to-day human practices at individual and social levels, the urge for a situation free from conflicts and struggles is derived here. Generally, a situation free from tension, struggle, dispute or conflict, particularly in socio-economic spheres, is considered the state of peace in this context. This phenomenon signifies the absence of fight or war between or among the nations and is generally the accepted notion of peace at the international level. It is almost the same in the Indian perspective. Popular Hindi words, which are derived from *Samskrit*, such as *Vishram*, *Nivriti*, *Nistabdha* and *Ananda* are used to describe a state of peace.

Despite this similarity between the Western and Indian perspectives, peace is not a motionless state even according to ancient philosophical thought. Peace is not a situation of the status quo. The state of peace provides man the pathway to progress in a tension-free atmosphere. Within a state of peace, efforts are made for healthy co-existence to extend the welfare of the people. Therefore, the state of peace is in fact dynamic. It fills people with enthusiasm and inspires them to move forward.

Education and Peace

Evidently education is the basis for the all-round development of man; it is the means of developing his personality. Moreover, it is the process that helps make one's life purposeful. All constructive and welfaristic conditions that may be required for the purpose are also inherent in this process. Similarly, peace, despite a state free from dispute, conflict and war, is also an active and dynamic state in which there is a call to go forward. New benefits are expected in a state of peace. It is the pathway to progress without any fear and confusion. Therefore, one can say that education and peace are linked to one-another. They supplement each other as both contribute to the development and welfare of each and every human being on this planet.

Gandhian View

According to Mahatma Gandhi, education is an unending exercise [filled with devotion-*Sadhana*][2] till death. For him, only education can act as a means to a successful life. Likewise, ***"education can help mould and shape the human body, mind and character in such a manner that they may act as the means to achieve joy and efficiency."***[3]

Categorically, education as expounded through Gandhi's imagination and explanation is a means to guide and lead a human-being from his birth to death. It helps man achieve his goal. The goal however, according to many philosophies including the *Vedic*-Hindu, could be the attainment of the *Mukti* or *Moksha*, or *Nirvana* [liberation] that it is considered as the highest stage of peace.

Furthermore, the imagination and explanation of Mahatma Gandhi about education could be better comprehended by the following statement of Kishorelal Mashruwala[4]:

"[This] ***works for the all-round growth of man right from the beginning till the end. Its ultimate aim is to turn human knowledge into his ability. It is for the purpose of making his life worthy and meaningful, and it is not only for earning his livelihood.***"[5]

Mahatma Gandhi wrote many articles on education from time-to-time. On several occasions, besides addressing students and teachers, he issued worthy statements regarding its meaning, purpose and importance in life. We can draw the following viewpoint particularly for the purpose of this short article:

1. The prime aim of education is to make a man self-dependent;

2. The purpose of education is to make the one efficient and skilful; and

3. The objective of education is to guide and lead him to the pathway to progress in the prevailing situation of space and as per the demand of time so that he could ascertain his physical and mental development to achieve a goal in life for himself on the one hand and he could equally contribute to the society, nation and the globe on the other.

After analyzing the above three points, it can be said with certainty that the Gandhian concept of education is one of the most important views on the subject for us today. This concept urges for man to be self-dependent, skilful and efficient. Thereby, his goal and objective, to achieve true education will be open. Not only this, the Gandhian view of education can play the vital role in the establishment of peace not only at the national level but also at the international level.

References:

1. The six *Vedangas* are in fact the six auxiliary disciplines traditionally associated with the study and understanding of the *Vedas* [four in number]. They are *Shiksha*, *Kalpa* [ritual], *Vyakarna* [grammar], *Nirukta* [etymology], *Chhandas* [meter] and *Jyotisha* [astronomy].

2. For, he used the words *Akhand Sadhana*. Particularly, the word *Sadhana* has a broad and deep meaning; besides being important in human life, it is a well-known concept in Indian philosophy. *Saadhana*: [साधना], in fact, is also the way or a means of accomplishing something through spiritual practice, which includes not only a variety of disciplines of the *Vedic*-Hindu tradition, [but] also the Jain, Buddhist and Sikh traditions followed in order to achieve certain spiritual objectives, or ultimately the *Moksha* or *Nirvana* [salvation], the goal of human life.

3. Essays on Gandhism and Peace, page 10

4. Kishorlal Mashruwala [1890-1952], a freedom fighter, Gandhian scholar and thinker was the editor of Harijan weekly started by the Mahatma.

5. Essays on Gandhism and Peace, page 10

Bibliography:

- Bhave, Vinoba. 1973. *Vinoba on Gandhi*. Wardha [India]: Sarva Sewa Sangh.

- Carter, Candice and Kumar, Ravindra. 2010. *Peace Philosophy in Action.* New York [USA]: Palgrave Macmillan.
- Gandhi, MK. 1927. *An Autobiography or the Story of My Experiments with Truth.* Ahmedabad [India]: Navajiva Publishing House.
- Gandhi, MK. 1957. *India of My Dreams.* Ahmedabad [India]: Navajivan Publishing House.
- Kumar, Ravindra. 1999. *Essays on Gandhism and Peace.* Meerut [India]: Krishna Publication.

*****

6

Gandhian Concept of Woman-Education: An Analysis

"As for women's education...I am strongly of opinion that women should have the same facilities as men and even special facilities where necessary."

–MK Gandhi

"Learning is a never ending constant process. It moulds human body, mind intellect and character to those tendencies which are key to bliss and efficiency."

–MK Gandhi

The above short statement of an anarchist and humanist like Mahatma Gandhi on education well elucidates his views on this important field. Not only at the world level but also at national level in India a section of intellectuals, despite accepting Gandhi as a great man does not consider him to be an educationist. Furthermore, the Mahatma is not considered an eminent intellectual in the academic sense of term, or a great scholar. However, above quoted lines illustrate what a great educationist and thinker Gandhi was? Not only this, he says, ***"I hold that true education of the intellect can only come through a proper exercise and training of the bodily organs, e.g. hands, feet, eyes, ears, nose, etc. In other words, an intelligent use of the bodily organs in a child provides the best and quickest way of developing his intellect. But unless the development of the mind and body goes hand in hand with a corresponding awakening of the soul, the former alone would prove to be a poor lop-sided affair."*** [Harijan, May 5, 1937]

And also this, ***"In India...where more than eighty percent of the population is agricultural and another ten percent industrial, it is a crime to make education merely literary, and to uplift boys and girls for manual work in after-life. Indeed I hold that as the larger part of our time***

is devoted to labour for earning our bread; our children must from their infancy be taught the dignity of such labour. There is no reason why a peasant's son after having gone to school becomes useless, as he does become..." [Young India, September 1, 1921]

Hence, it is clear that Gandhi's views on education are logical. They seem matured, important and worthy. They are not of the least importance when compared to the views of any of his contemporary educationists. Moreover, Gandhi himself had been one of the most excellent educationists of his time. Regarding meaning and purpose of education, he was quite clear. He was also clear about making education purposeful, a perfect means for all-round development of personality as it could be observed from his above statements. His suggestions to make education valuable and prophesying were, and are, worthy of consideration. They were, and are, adaptable in current perspectives and will remain so in future in their refined form as per the demand of time and space.

Women Education

When Gandhi talks of education or he discusses the merit of education, or hopes general welfare through it, he not only includes women in the learning fold, but lays great stress on their participation in the entire process of education. To quote Gandhi himself, ***"As for women's education...I am strongly of opinion that women should have the same facilities as men and even special facilities where necessary."*** [India of My Dreams, page 201][1]

Along with this, Gandhi was seriously concerned of

pervasive illiteracy among Indians and particularly about lack of education in women. He was fully conscious of women's contribution in the building of society and nation and for their role in national liberation movement. Thus, he was committed to women education and that is why, he went to the extent of saying, ***"There should be night schools for illiterate [particularly women] adults...they must be helped to acquire general knowledge through lectures..."*** [India of My Dreams, page 201]

Gandhi's commitment to women education can also be observed from his sincere desire of providing them rights equivalent to men. He was not ready to accept an argument of denying rights to women on the ground of their illiteracy, or lack of education. He was not prepared for depriving women of their rights on the ground of their backwardness. However, he was of the firm opinion that education was essential for women enabling them to protect their rights and, simultaneously, to improve their condition. In Gandhi's own words, ***"Education is essential for enabling women to uphold...rights. Propagation of education among millions of women is inevitable for their progress."*** [Essays on Gandhism and Peace, page 4]

Moreover, his sincerity could be well understood finally from the following statement, which, besides Gandhi's concern over women education, clarifies the importance and significance of his views in this regard, ***"Despite not being identical, man and woman are of equal rank. They are a peerless pair being supplementary to one another; each helps the other, so that without the one the existence of the other***

cannot be conceived, and therefore, it follows as a necessary corollary from these facts that anything that will impair the status of either of them will involve the equal ruin of them both."

Hence, he quite clearly puts forward, ***"In framing any scheme of women's education this cardinal truth must be constantly kept in mind."*** [India of My Dreams, page 231][2]

Arguments in Favour of Women Education

From the time immemorial, education has played a vital role in making human life prosperous and worthy. In its refined form education has guided humanity at all levels and in all walks of life for its betterment as per the demand of time and space. From time-to-time many thinkers, scholars, philosophers and great men all over the world have accorded dimensions to the field of education. Indeed, Mahatma Gandhi is one of them. His views, opinions and arguments, particularly in context of women education, are still relevant. A ray of hope appears in them for those countless illiterate women all over the world who due to the lack of education are suppressed. Hence, Gandhi's views on women education become worthy of consideration. They demand their careful study and critical analysis. But, side-by-side, throwing a glance at two of his following extraordinary arguments for women education will be appropriate:

- Education is the means of all-round development of personality; it is an endless process, starting from the early age and continuing till death, for achieving goal of life. The beginning of learning takes place from one's home, i.e., depends upon mother's efforts. Despite numerous fundamental changes in social and cultural spheres, it is still true not only in Indian perspectives but in context of the whole Asia. Families are still important. Role of women, as the centre of family affairs, remains vital. They maintain their supremacy there. Therefore, literacy and education among women and that too on priority is essential. In this regard, Gandhi's argument seems to be based on truth. Moreover, his stress on imparting equal equation among women, and on giving priority to them where necessary, also seems to be realistic; and

- Education is the best means of self-development, and self-development is a fundamental right of all, men and women. Hence, it is essential that women should be educated. They acquire knowledge equivalent to men. Mahatma Gandhi was of the opinion that until and unless women, on the basis of education and knowledge do not find their proper place in social and economic fields, they could not achieve self-respect for themselves. Nor they could become self-dependent in any of the walks of life. He had said so in context of the whole world in general and India in particular. We know that his experiences related to it were based on real condition of Indian women, and particularly those belonged to rural areas.

Particularly in Indian contexts, Mahatma Gandhi had said, ***"I am quite conscious of the fact that in the villages generally they [women] hold their own; ...and in some matters they rule. But...the legal and customary status***

of women is bad enough throughout and demands radical alternation." [Essays on Gandhism and Peace, page 5]. For this, he had further said, ***"Despite the legislation their awareness is important and essential."*** [Essays on Gandhism and Peace, page 3]

Analysis

Undoubtedly, in context of women education both the above arguments of the Mahatma were based on truth. They were important in his lifetime on the one hand and are of worth consideration in current perspective on the other. Particularly, in a country like India where literacy rate among women is quite low and propagation of education in them is absolutely necessary. For example, in some parts of north India women are still illiterate up to ninety percent in many communities. How such women could get equality in society? How could those totally illiterate and uneducated women become guide for their children? And, it is a fact that families who have such women are comparatively backward in all walks of life, including socio-economic. They are far behind than others in political field and their cultural progress is a matter of serious concern.

In his lifetime Gandhi inspired Indians to take concrete and practical initiatives regarding women education. In the root of them were the following two purposes:

- Advancement in knowledge; and
- Self-sufficiency in social and economic fields

As we have already learnt, the purpose of filling women with knowledge and imparting education in them was to bring them out of those centuries' old conservative customs and rules, which were responsible for their mental and social slavery. Gandhi was clearly of the opinion, ***"Woman has been suppressed under custom and law for which man was responsible and in shaping of which she had no hand."***

In such a situation it is not so easy for a woman to become free. She cannot come out of this state and break the shackles immediately. For, it is necessary that she receives equal opportunity for the making of self, and it is possible through her advancement in knowledge. A wise woman can transform the attitude of man. She has the capacity to do so. In Mahatma Gandhi's words, ***"They can win over the tendency of man who consider themselves to be lords and masters [of women]."***

In this context Gandhi was also of the opinions [Constructive Programme, page 17] that in their conscious state of mind or in their advancement in knowledge, women can become free from the yoke of any kind of slavery, individual or social.

The sole purpose behind making women self-sufficient in social and economic fields is to obtain equality through self efforts on the one hand and to ascertain their participation particularly in these spheres on the other. In this regard, Gandhi's stress on women's association with constructive programmes is significant. Many initiatives regarding women education, and side-by-side their participation in constructive programmes, have been taken in India after Gandhi passed away. Some of those programmes are still on and they demand their fair analysis to prove relevance of Mahatma Gandhi's views on women education.

References:

1. In this regard he was committed to impart fourfold education among women. In his plan of such kind of education, besides general education [as per the syllabus set for the purpose] and moral teaching, essentially include physical and technical learning. [Essays on Gandhism and Peace, page 2-5]

2. Accepting men's supremacy in the outward activities Mahatma Gandhi went to the extent of saying, ***"Home life is entirely the sphere of woman and, therefore, in the upbringing and education of children, women ought to have more knowledge..."***

Bibliography:

- Gandhi, MK. 1957. *An Autobiography or the Story of My Experiments with Truth*. Ahmedabad [India]: Navajivan Publishing House.
- Gandhi, MK [ed.]. 1933-41, 1942-8. *Harijan Weekly*. Ahmedabad [India]: Harijan Sewak Sangh and Navajivan Trust.
- Gandhi, MK. 1957. *India of My Dreams*. Ahmedabad [India]: Navajivan Publishing House.
- Gandhi, MK [ed.]. 1919-31. *Young India Weekly*. [Reprinted in 13 Volumes in 1984]. Ahmedabad [India]: Navajivan Publishing House.
- Kumar, Ravindra. 1999. *Essays on Gandhism and Peace*. Meerut [India]: Krishna Publications.
- Kumar, Ravindra. 2006. *Gandhian Thoughts: An Overview*. New Delhi [India]: Gyan Publishing House.

*****

7

The Gandhian Way: A Universal Method of Resolving Conflicts

"When a person claims to be non-violent, he is expected not to be angry with one who has injured him. He will not wish him harm; he will wish him well; he will not swear at him; he will not cause any physical hurt. He will put up with all the injury to which he is subjected by the wrong-doer. Thus non-violence is complete innocence. Complete non-violence is complete absence of ill-will against all that lives. It therefore embrace sub-human life not excluding noxious insects or beasts...Non-violence is therefore in its active good-will towards all life, it is the pure love..."

-MK Gandhi

Introduction

The word conflict is basically derived from *conflictus* of *Latin*. In fact it appeared in the English vocabulary at the end of the Fourteenth Century or in the early years of the Fifteenth Century AD. The basic idea in the root of this word is disharmony, generally between two individuals or groups of individuals who indulge in violence-based activities to serve their interest; for this, they continuously try to establish their superiority on others by different means or ways.

In Indian terms conflict is *Takrav*, which is near to *Sangharsh*, a word that has basically originated from *Samskrit* –one of the oldest and the soundest languages of the world. As this word is found in the oldest texts of this language; in *Vedic*-Hindu treatises, it is evident that it is an old word. Further, when an analysis of this word is made minutely, it categorically appears that it is a struggle [*sangharsh*] –generally between two opposite parties [individuals or groups] who come face-to-face with the purpose of their respective victory. They fight with one-another; each one of them tries to establish superiority on the other.

Hence, there is almost unanimity between the Western and the Indian views pertaining to conflict, its meaning and general idea in its root.

Inevitability of Conflicts: Some Related Facts

After becoming familiar with the meaning and getting a general idea of the root of the word conflict, it is now necessary to keep in mind some undeniable facts pertaining to conflict before getting into further discussion over the subject in hand.

First: Conflicts are necessary in life; they are inevitable in human society. Their evaporation in toto from man's life and society is almost impossible. Thinkers and scholars of repute, social scientists and sociologists in particular, have thus declared them as inevitable fact of social experience.[1] Besides this, the study and analysis of religious scriptures or texts, and histories related to them, also categorically reveal this fact. Therefore, it must be borne in mind that conflicts are a necessity or inevitability of society; their complete disappearance from life and society is impossible.

Second: With the constantly growing process of human development, the scope of conflicts has also expanded simultaneously. The study and analysis of the entire human history also compel us to agree to this reality. In the continuous process of increasing population and progress at different levels of all walks of life, conflicts have also multiplied. Further, in this process, the nature of conflicts and their effects on life and society have also definitely changed. As this process continues to move, the dynamics of human life is also expanding, indicating that the state of conflict will never evaporate entirely.

Conflict is a subject indivisibly connected to human development. In other words, it has essentially been with the process of man's progress and it will remain so in future.

Therefore, a question could be raised, why is this so? Answer to this is quite clear and factual.

The unprecedented evolution of the human species categorically makes us familiar with man's attributes of expansive comprehension. The human being uses intellect with intuition, thus turning it into wisdom –the higher key of his true nature as expanded being. The expanded individual becomes aware of his greater dynamics within the scope of life, and hence, blissfully provides a position of great honour and gains a place of esteem on the earthly plane. An individual using intellect with wisdom is indeed extraordinary and his impact is great.

Despite the presence of *Ahimsa* permanently in man's nature, in the process of his progress, jealousy and competition, the two temporary tendencies, which are also inherent, get enlarged. They then give birth to selfishness, appetite, violence and passion, and rapidly enhance the potency of these two tendencies. To satisfy his desires, man wishes to go ahead of others at all levels and in all walks of life. So, he tries to become the master of others, which generates the state of conflict.

Thus, the emergence and increase in the state of conflict could be attributed to man's longing for selfishness – narrowness in outlook leading him to fear and distrust and creates grounds for disharmony. In this context, man always has two options at his disposal. One is to overcome those temporary tendencies, which give birth to the state of conflict and to step forward courageously for harmony; in the other to steer the cause of disharmony for attaining selfish motives. Generally, people adhere to the later. They stretch it to an extent that it aggravates trouble and gets transformed into conflicts of serious nature, be it at the local, regional, national level, or even war at the international level. The contrary state, which can be transformed to harmony by intellect, firm determination and true ability at the individual level, at the beginning worsens and becomes untoward.

All thinkers and scholars of the past or the present, from the East and the West, in one way or the other, arrive at the same conclusion. In India, Bhishma[2] –a known character of the *Mahabharata* declares *Adharma* to be the root cause of conflicts in society, which originates from human tendencies. Similarly, Vishnugupta Chanakya[3] –an eminent Indian thinker of ancient time declares social inequality and people's self-interest, both related to human tendencies, as being the cause of conflicts. It is a long chain comprising thinkers not only from ancient, medieval or contemporary periods, but from the modern period as well.

From the West whether it is Aristotle[4] –one of the greatest Greek philosophers of ancient period, or a leading Christian thinker like Thomas Aquinas[5]; whether it is Niccolò di Bernardo dei Machiavelli[6], from medieval age, or a contemporary classical German thinker like Georg Wilhelm Friedrich Hegel[7], or Karl Marx[8], all of them in one way or the other accept that conflicts originate from human tendencies. Further, people associated with known theories, or studies, analysis and researches on subjects related to security, peace and conflict that particularly emerged in the West during the

Nineteenth and the Twentieth Centuries, including Herbert Spencer [1820, April 27–1903, December 8], Edward Said [1935, November 1–2003, September] Frantz Fanon [1925, July 20–1961, December 6], Talcott Parsons [1902, December 13–1979, May 8], Kingsley Davis [1908, August 20–1997, February 27], William Moore [1864, November 22–1944, November 28], Robert Merton [1910, July 4–2003, February 23], Gabriel Almond [1911, January 12–2002, December 25], Andre Frank [1929, February 24–2005, April 23], Immanuel Wallenstein [1930, September 28] and Volker Bornschier [1944] also accept this reality. All of them, accept that social inequality –a state in which an individual or a group, or groups of individuals do not have equal status in the society, lack political rights such as the right to vote, freedom of speech or expression, property or wealth, education, health and suffer discrimination in the name of caste, class, ethnicity, gender or race, and also confront denial of social justice, act as the central point of conflicts and indicate towards those human tendencies that are responsible for the emergence of such a state.

Moreover, Ludwing Gumplowicz[9] and Laster Frank Ward[10] –the two most eminent sociologists from the West –also accept those tendencies, which are in my opinion temporary in man, as sources that provoke individuals and groups to establish superiority over others and thus, to give birth to conflicts. This reality could also be observed clearly from the following statement of Rudolph J Rummel [1932] –a renowned professor and political scientist of the Hawaii University [USA]:

"Conflict is a balancing of powers among interests, capabilities, and wills. It is a mutual adjusting of what people want, can get, and are willing to pursue. Conflict behaviour whether hostile actions, violence, or war, is then a means and manifestation of this process."

Third: Despite the necessity of conflicts in man's life, what we need to accept further is that, right from the time of emergence of conflicts, efforts for their resolution were also initiated. Particularly, on the basis of the natural, eternal and supreme human value of *Ahimsa*, the process of transformation of conflicts [or struggles] into cooperation was also started. Interestingly, this *Ahimsa*-based process always recorded victory over the violent-originated state, eventually transforming the state of conflict in one way or the other into cooperation. It is a reality. If the atmosphere of cooperation was not created, the process of development would never go forward. So, this unprecedented development would have never become apparent. If the state of cooperation would not emerge, human race would extinct long ago, to say in the very beginning. In this regard, the following statement of Mahatma Gandhi is worth quoting here:

"If mankind was not...non-violent, it would have self-destroyed ages ago. But in the duel between forces of violence and non-violence the later has always come out victorious in the end."[11]

It should be borne firmly in mind that the process of emergence of conflicts in society and their resolution, or struggles and their transformation will continue. This is in fact a subject, which is inextricably linked to human existence on the one hand and their development on the other. Therefore, it will continue until human beings exist and the process of development goes on; also, bearing the truth firmly in mind that harmony and balance are not only needed for existence, but also for the continuation of the process of development. Stepping forward always remained necessary and will always be so bolstered by concrete thinking and action that challenges the prevailing situations. For the inevitability of harmony and balance, efforts for resolving conflicts, as has been mentioned already, can never be given up.

Historical Context

A huge number of pages of human history is before us, which reflect stories pertaining to tensions, clashes-conflicts, struggles and wars at regional, national and international levels. People are seen in indulging in wars, not only for years or decades[12], but in some cases continuously for centuries.[13] History also shows as to how people try to establish superiority over others and also depicts the way in which they exploit their fellow beings.

What more the pages of history disclose is how after fighting severely for years and decades and after a heavy loss of life and wealth, involved and affected parties got tired. It remained as the truth undoubtedly for all those involved-affected. Not only for those who were weak or defenders, but it was for those also who were mighty, invaders or aggressors.[14] They took the course of dialogues-negotiations and subsequently entered into agreements, compromises or treaties, and stopped fights and wars. For this, as and when required, they also sought the support of others through arbitration. Thus, they clearly adopted measures, which were based on non-violence and through this, they tried to prevent the state emerged of violence. The whole process pertaining to dialogues-negotiations, compromises and treaties is within the scope of non-violence. This is the only way to stop or prevent conflicts, fights or wars, and there is no other alternative to it.

Despite being mighty and stronger in position in comparison to the opponent, or even after establishing one's victory over the weak, the mighty or victorious one, realizing the fact that there was no other way available except to adopt the process of dialogue, compromise and treaty, had always taken recourse to this. This is the only reality.

Universal Process of Conflict Resolution

We must firmly bear in our mind and heart that the fact related to inevitability of conflicts and their resolution through the way or method discussed already, which has been applied through the ages and which is applied even in current perspective, or will be applied in future, is not confined to the global context, or in other words in context of this planet only. It would have similarly been applied, is applied and will be applied in case of conflicts and their resolution on other planets of the universe also, where there may be existence of other developed beings. This is a reality pertaining to the universe; undoubtedly, this is a universal process. In this regard, there may not be other alternative to this. I can venture to repeat it again, if there is the existence of human beings on any other planet, the reality about inevitability of conflicts and the way of their resolution is the same. The universal law of balance and harmony works everywhere in the galaxy, it is a building block of our existence, from the spiritual to the scientific to the pragmatic. That is why; the word universal has been added to the title of discussion in hand.

Gandhian Perspective

After accepting the reality of conflicts in men's life, their source of emergence and continuous efforts, which human beings have been making through the ages for their resolution, now, we shall come to the subject in hand – *The Gandhian Way to Resolve Conflicts*.

The Gandhian method as a way of conflict resolution has existed for over a century. It has not only been a subject of people's attraction, but, it has affected so many fundamental changes, particularly in political sphere all over the world. Due to its uniqueness, it is still the nucleus among all the methods available for the purpose. It establishes superiority, particularly over those, whose fundamental way itself is based on violence. Further, as Gandhian method possesses all possibilities of resolving conflicts in a fine and peaceful manner if adopted in its refined form as per the demand of time and space, its analysis becomes indispensable. Let us, therefore, discuss its worth and adaptability, having its foremost features in the centre!

Meaning and Basic Spirit in the Root of Gandhian Way

Gandhian is a word associated undoubtedly with Gandhi –the Mahatma. This word categorically reveals exemplary and matchless characteristics of Gandhi's personality. Besides illuminating what Gandhi did and thought in the larger interest and welfare of humanity, the word Gandhian simultaneously inspires others also to do and think for the sake of humanity. For example: when it is said of an individual that he is a Gandhian, it immediately and definitely reminds of those unique characteristics that were the part and parcel of life of Mohandas Karamchand Gandhi. Further, it is also deduced that the person who is being termed as Gandhian is necessarily in agreement with the pathway shown by Mahatma Gandhi. Same thing applies to a particular job completed or attempted at completion by an individual or individuals at any level in accordance with the views or ideas of the Mahatma. This can be a general explanation for the word Gandhian and the spirit of its root.

Basis of Gandhian Method

Ahimsa [non-violence] is the basis of the Gandhian method or Gandhism, which is a blend of the views and practices of Mohandas Karamchand Gandhi. This reality could categorically be observed just from a short statement of the Mahatma himself in which he says, ***"Truth is my religion*** [*Dharma*] ***and Ahimsa*** [non-violence] ***is the only way of its realization."***[15]

It could also be realized from his following statement:

"I will not sacrifice Truth and Ahimsa even for the deliverance of my country **or** ***religion."***[16]

And:

"My love for non-violence is superior to that for every other thing –mundane or supramundane. It is equaled only by love for Truth, which is to me synonymous with non-violence; through which and which alone I can see and reach Truth."[17]

Moreover, from all of the actions that Mahatma Gandhi took recourse for the purpose of seeking justice for thousands of Asians, Indians in particular in South Africa, and later for the freedom of *crores* of his fellow countrymen in India, between 1917 and 1947, his commitment to *Ahimsa* could categorically be observed. As is known, he remained firm towards *Ahimsa* despite suffering atrocities in South Africa. Not only this, on his part he was never found wanting in showing immediate regret for any of the acts that could be termed as violent and thus immoral.

It was Gandhi who after a violent incident at Chauri-Chaura[18] in February, 1922, suddenly stopped the Non-Cooperation Movement, when it seemed to be in its definitive stage, because of the entry of violence in the action. He not only regretted for it, but also acknowledged that it was a Himalayan blunder on his part.

From that incident Gandhi realized that people's judgment of the opponent was an equal act of violence. Therefore, he took this act as being against the basic spirit of non-violence.

Not to stand in the opposite is the basic spirit of *Ahimsa*. True love for one and all always prevails in it. For, *Ahimsa* acquires a neutral attitude; disarming both sides in one wisdom moment. This is the universal law of allowance and thus resulted in true balance, which Gandhi applied. Such was his pledge and dedication to non-violence as a practice.

His commitment to non-violence could also be well observed from his refusal to support the English in the World War Second in 1939, even though the Colonialists were ready to promise to grant freedom to India immediately after the War in return. In Gandhi's view act like this was in fact violation of his ideal and steadfast principle of *Ahimsa*, which could be equated with act of supporting the British in violence at the international level for the deliverance of the country.[19]

It was the chief quality of his individual self that what he said or preached of *Ahimsa*, he himself tried to practice. Uniformity, approximately if not completely, between ideas and practices was the foremost characteristic of Gandhi's personality. In the entire human history a few could be listed in this regard.

Ahimsa [Non-Violence]

Having familiarity with Gandhi's commitment to *Ahimsa*, in theory and practice, it is necessary to know in brief the general idea of *Ahimsa* on the one hand and the Gandhian viewpoint pertaining to non-violence on the other.

Generally, ***'not to hurt any living being by one's own thought, utterance or deed, and not to kill or cause to for...'*** is *Ahimsa*.[20]

Moreover, the scope of *Ahimsa* is free of tension and conflict. It is full of harmony and balance. In place of tension, acceptance prevails. From the basic spirit of non-violence, unity and peace are created.

Gandhi, agreeing to this, stresses on making ***"intent underlying the act the acid text of Himsa*** [violence] ***or Ahimsa*** [non-violence]***"***[21]

For a clarification of the view of Gandhi, his own following statement is worth quoting here:

"When a person claims to be non-violent, he is expected not to be angry with one who has injured him. He will not wish him harm; he will wish him well; he will not swear at him; he will not cause any physical hurt. He will put up with all the injury to which he is subjected by the wrong-doer. Thus non-violence is complete innocence. Complete non-violence is complete absence of ill-will against all that lives. It therefore embrace sub-human life not excluding noxious insects or beasts...Non-violence is therefore in its active good-will towards all life, it is the pure love..."[22]

This proclamation of the Mahatma, besides making his viewpoint of *Ahimsa* important and significant, also divulges the following two things:

1. *Ahimsa* is a subject related to mind and spirit; and
2. It is an act; therefore, a matter of practice.

Thus, categorically, *Ahimsa* relates to mind and action, both. However, its fundamental source is the human nature.

Man ultimately realizes it, longs for it, cultivates it and on the basis of it, steps forward for cooperation. That is why; I have time and again mentioned in my various writings and lectures particularly on topics related to it that *Ahimsa* is a natural value.[23] This is the first and the supreme human value; the *Janni* of morality[24], or as many scholars have rightly described, it is the highest form of morality in itself. And, that is why; after disputes, conflicts, fights or wars, it has always been taken as the basis of their resolution in various forms, dialogues-negotiations, compromises or treaties. It remains so till today and will be in all times to come. Further, this reality, not applies to the earth only, but as an essential condition of existence, progress and achievement of goals, which is unparalleled and the most effective method of conflict resolution, also applies in any of the planets of the universe, where there may be the presence of man.[25]

Mahatma Gandhi, thus, chose a wonderful *Ahimsa*-based way. Moreover, as mentioned already, by making intent underlying the act as the acid test of *Ahimsa*, Gandhi on the one hand accorded a unique dimension to it both in theory and practice, on the other hand the Mahatma ascertained success in the actions that he initiated either in South Africa or in India. With this, many others also adopted the Gandhian way in different parts of the world for seeking justice, freedom and equality. They applied it in prevailing situations of space and time, and recorded unprecedented success on the basis of it. It has indeed, remained exemplary in the whole human history. Hopefully, it remains important for the present and will be so in all times to come, if it is taken in its refined form by those wishing justice, freedom and equality.

Analysis of Actions

Undoubtedly, the *Ahimsa*-based Gandhian way or the method remains till today significant and adaptable in resolving conflicts, or to the solution to various socio-political, economic, ideological or cultural problems. It will be so in future as well. That is why; the analysis of the actions of the Mahatma himself, and of those others who adopted his method or the way in their respective actions, becomes necessary. In this chain first of all, a brief discussion about the series of events related to South Africa, where for the first time in the whole human history Gandhi took initiatives in political sphere on the basis of highest human value of *Ahimsa* may be considered. In South Africa, he indeed more or less achieved success and thus showed a way to be followed by one and all to establish justice at any level and anywhere in the world.

The development and application of Gandhi's ideas in South Africa could be understood in two phases:

The first is between 1893 and 1901 and second from 1902 and 1914. In the first what could be observed categorically is:

- To realize injustice, in other words self-awakening towards the wrong;
- To take pledge of not bowing to injustice by self, and to step forward to save others too from it;

- To make constant endeavours towards creating awakening among those affected, and to obtain their cooperation for the establishment of justice;
- To win support of those others who are ready to favour the cause imbued with truth and for this willingly prepared to extend assistance and cooperation for the restoration of justice;[26]
- To select carefully those preliminary methods that could seem appropriate and effective in prevailing situation of space and time;
- To enter to the course of action through the selected methods –to make request orally and/or in written in the form of applications, memorandums, dialogues, demonstrations and resistances –gradually until and unless injustice is not eliminated.[27]

Similarly in the second phase what could be experienced is:

- To maintain full courage continuously and further pledging for not bowing before injustice;
- To be ready to bear any kind of atrocity, individually or collectively, including imprisonment;
- To gather and inspire people for constructive works with the purpose of their unity and self-reliance, and ascertain their collective participation in action;
- To take the course of active means like that of boycott, non-cooperation, resistance, non-payment of unjust

dues, or the one that could be fit and efficient in existing situation of space and time; and

- To have the action continue until and unless the purpose is fulfilled; problem is resolved, in other words, justice is established.[28]

Hence, *Ahimsa*-based Gandhian way for the first time developed in two phases in South Africa. It is generally known as the passive non-violent resistance for the reason that methods like *request*, *plea*, *petition* or *submission of memorandum*, were there in the course. But, in fact, those courses cannot be termed as passive. They were, and are, the steps of non-violent resistance and struggle for justice and freedom. Moreover, when action was there, how the application of the word passive would be appropriate for such courses? In reality, those steps were, and still are essentially connected to the Gandhian method. They are the fundamentals to pave the way for furthering the cause; therefore, they are always important and significant, if adopted in consonance of prevailing situation.

In India, as is known, the purpose of Gandhi's actions was different from South Africa. Along with getting justice and freedom, the upliftment of fellow countrymen was also the purpose of Gandhi's actions in India. Bringing Indians out of their slave-like mentality and getting them realized of their past glory, and ascertaining equality for compatriots was the spirit in root of Gandhi's actions. Moreover, he viewed that Indians must stand up and fight against injustice on the basis of highest human value of *Ahimsa*. Thus, by ensuring their own freedom and equality, they should pave the way for the welfare, prosperity and progress of each and everyone on this planet.

Gandhi returned back to India in 1915 from South Africa and immediately he started observing the prevailing situation of the country. Along with participating in some of the public activities, he tried to establish direct contact with people, particularly the rural masses. In the years 1917-8, he launched two actions at the local levels –in Champaran [Bihar] and Kheda [Gujarat] with the purpose of attaining justice for the peasantry, which was, and is, the soul of India. The peasantry is the backbone of rural India and real development of the country till today depends on *crores* of hardworking farmers.

After these two local level events, Gandhi launched three nationwide mass actions: the Non-Cooperation [1920], the Civil Disobedience [1930] and the Quit India [1942]. The purpose of these three was to awaken the slumbering fellow countrymen and bringing them out of their slave-like mentality. Besides, the aim was also to make the people realized the importance of freedom and equality in life, and thus to ascertain their active participation on the basis of *Ahimsa* in the national cause. Further, to make them realized that freedom and justice are connected to each other, therefore, without compromising for these two, to step forward for the well being of one and all.

In this regard, Gandhi along with an excellent team of other leaders stepped forward. He conveying to the people of India emphatically the message of becoming completely free of any kind of mental slavery and by staying within the scope of morality to take the following steps in non-violent fight for freedom in particular:

- Boycott the foreign-made goods; boycott schools, colleges, universities and judiciary under the control of the Colonial Government, and to adopt *Swadeshi*;[29]
- Not to cooperate with the system, and to take the course of civil disobedience as the furthering step, which included non-payment of all taxes and refusal of all unjust laws; and
- Stepping forward continuously with a firm determination of doing or dying until and unless the goal is not achieved.

Along with this, other front-ranking leaders from the team of Gandhi –Vallabhbhai Patel [1875, October 31-1950, December 15], Jawaharlal Nehru [1889, November 14-1964, May 27], Abdul Ghaffar Khan [1898-1988, January 20][30] and Chakravarti Rajagopalachari [1878, December 10-1972, December 25][31] in particular, having local-regional issues in dispute in the centre, launched actions for their resolution through non-violent means. For this, they made strategies that could be fit according to the prevailing circumstances of space, obtained people's support and cooperation. In some of these strategies, unprecedented successes were achieved, particularly in those where people remained committed to discipline, in maintaining unity and showing collective strength.[32]

Finally, India achieved her freedom from the British Colonial Rule under the leadership of Mahatma Gandhi on August 15, 1947. The actions launched by him for the purpose, and movements [*Satyagrahas*] conducted by others on the strength of *Ahimsa* were largely responsible for this great achievement. This was a unique and unprecedented event in the entire history of the world. This great event still remains matchless. There is no other example as this in the whole human history to compare it from the means [*Ahimsa*] viewpoint. Albert Einstein, the great scientist of the Twentieth Century and a contemporary of the Mahatma had declared:

"Mahatma Gandhi's life achievement stands unique in political history. He has invented a completely new and humane means for the liberation war of an oppressed country, and practiced it with greatest energy and devotion. The moral influence he had on the consciously thinking human being of the entire civilized world will probably be much more lasting than it seems in our time with its overestimation of brutal violence forces. Because lasting will only is the work of such statesman who wake up and strengthen the moral power of their people through their example and educational work."[33]

For this, Einstein had gone to the extent of saying:

"Generations to come...will scarcely believe that such a one as this even in flesh and blood walked upon this earth." [34]

Through this, *crores* of people obtained freedom and

justice from one of the mightiest empires of the world –the British Empire. A new and noble *Ahimsa*-based way could open to resolve problem, dispute or conflict –especially in the political sphere.

Gandhi, who fought for truth –freedom, equality and justice on the basis of *Ahimsa*, for the solution of political problems, he took recourse to strategies during his actions in South Africa. Later, his colleagues and he planned and applied strategies as art to ascertain success in non-violent actions in India. Particularly, excellent and effective strategies were made in the Nagpur Flag *Satyagraha* [1923] and the Bardoli *Kisan* Agitation [1928] respectively, and they played important role in their success.

Not only in Gandhi's lifetime, but even after his passing away, these strategies remain significant and effective in non-violent actions, especially in the United States. These strategies, if well-planned and also prepared according to the demand of time, are still important and adaptable, and fully capable of ascertaining success.

By adhering to non-violent means, those malicious policies or steps were made unsuccessful in a planned way, which were, or were to be taken by Colonialists with the purpose of denying justice to the people. For example: the sole purpose of strategies planned and applied in the Bardoli *Kisan* Agitation was to make the whole administration paralyzed on the strength of people's unity in toto so that the Colonial Government could yield to compromise. Moreover, they were to encounter non-violently those measures, which were being taken by the administration to make the agitation weak and futile.

Similarly, in response to those unjust measures, which were being taken by the Colonial Government to weaken the Civil Disobedience Movement even before its launch by Mahatma Gandhi in 1930, he chose the technique of marching slowly toward Dandi, 4-5 miles a day, with the purpose of mass awakening. Further, reaching Dandi, a coastal village in Surat District of Gujarat and breaking of the Salt Law there, was also a part of his strategy. Salt might seem a small issue from the point of view of economics, but due to its being an essential part of life of all, it was important and a salt-centred action could draw the attention of the whole nation. That is why; Gandhi chose this and through it he exhorted the people of India to attain justice and freedom from the alien rule.

His going to fast unto death against the declaration made by the British Premier Ramsey MacDonald in 1932 was also in my opinion a part of his strategy to compel the Colonialists to withdraw it. It was a declaration to divide the people of the country in the name of class and caste with the purpose of maintaining the Colonial hold over India. Gandhi's action of going to the fast unto death in the Yerawada Prison of Pune was, as said already, a part of his strategy, but it was at the same time related to a very important and gigantic national issue; therefore, he did not hesitate in taking a big risk of sacrificing even his life and he made it a part of his strategy. In fact, any non-violence-based task demands for a sacrifice simultaneously. This is the distinctiveness of the Gandhian way itself.

The actions started by the Afro-Americans in the sixth and the seventh decades of the Twentieth Century in the United States of America for equality and justice were influenced by the Gandhian ways. Prominent Gandhians to be reckoned here were: Martin Luther King Junior [1929, January 15-1968, April 4][35], Rosa Parks [1913, February 4-2005, October 24][36], Ralph David Abernathy Sr. [1926, March 11-1990, April 17][37], James Bevel [1939, October 19-2008, December 19][38] and more than three dozen others. They were committed to *Ahimsa*, through their well planned strategies, they stepped forward for equality and justice. For this, they kept themselves ready to bear any kind of atrocity or cruelty, and even to sacrifice their lives. This series of events pertaining to the Afro-Americans' resistance for justice was another milestone of the non-violent way –the Gandhian method.

In South Africa, the series of events, particularly the trust of Nelson Rolihlahla Mandela [1918, July 18] and his colleagues in the non-violent way and methods till the early years of the seventh decade of the Twentieth Century, their showing of indifference to non-violent means thereafter, and again in accepting this way in the last decade of the Century to be the most effective and welfaristic in restoring peace, and in establishing justice and equality, tell us a different story than the actions of the Afro-Americans in the United States. However, this also reveals the superiority of the non-violent way over all other methods available for the purpose, violence-based measures in particular. From the statement made by Nelson Mandela that *all differences can be resolved through the process of negotiation*, it becomes clear that the universal method of resolution is the one and the same, and it prevails always. There is no alternative to it.

Further what the series of events pertaining to South Africa reveals categorically is that the non-violent way demands patience and expects for sacrifice. If it was so and non-violent strategies would have been made as per the demand of time and space, Mandela and his colleagues would never stray from the non-violent way and methods. Risks as well as demand for self-sacrifice are always there in non-violent methods. This must be understood by those who desire resolution of conflicts through this noble *Ahimsa*-based way –the Gandhian way, or the universal method.

In this regard, one of the best examples in the form of the People's Power Revolution, also known as the *EDSA* [Epifanio de los Santos Avenue] *Revolution* and the *Yellow Revolution* respectively in the Philippines in 1986 is also before us. Through a good strategy a fundamental change in political sphere was brought through the non-violent method. For achieving the purpose –justice, through mass awakening, understanding and a few days [22-25 February] assembly of determined people on streets of Metropolitan Manila, who were ready to make sacrifice for the cause –change, an astonishing and exemplary success could be possible peacefully, non-violently.

The historical event of the Philippines reminds us time and again to become adherent to non-violent means, to have the patience when in action and to be ready to make sacrifice if there is a desire for success in resolving conflict, or wishing justice through peaceful or non-violent means.

Many other examples are also before us, such as the series of events of Vietnam, which prove that conflict can be resolved through non-violent means, if people plan strategies befitting to the prevailing circumstances, and step forward to action with patience, determination and a sense of sacrifice. The changes, which took place mostly through people's non-violent actions in the last three decades of the last century in the countries of the Eastern Europe like in Poland under the leadership of Lech Walesa [1943, September 29] could undoubtedly be counted in this chain.

The people of the Middle East are also waiting for fundamental changes in their respective countries. They are keen to get rid of centuries old dictatorships and military-rules, and for this they are struggling for years. But, they are, in fact, lacking able leadership and proper directions to bring about changes by non-violent methods. All possibilities are there in the Middle East for such changes. The universal method of resolving conflicts is equally effective, important and welfaristic for this region also, but for this they need well planned strategies and action plan befitting in prevailing situations of space, and as per the demand of time. If it is done properly, not much time would be required to root out centuries old hereditary dictatorships and military-rules, and thus to accord justice to people. To repeat, the people of the region lack understanding pertaining to the importance of non-violent way, its capacity of initiating fundamental changes, and its proper application. For equality, freedom and justice through this way they need to understand it; simultaneously, they need honest, able and selfless leaders who are firm, dedicated and ready to make sacrifice for the cause. Hopefully, it will take place there sooner or later!

Resolution Process and Steps

Although the Gandhian way in resolving conflicts or in settling disputes seems quite simple, but it is simultaneously abide by certain principles, which are the essentials of the moral structure of the universe. For this, having the life of Mahatma Gandhi in the centre, Martin Luther King Junior has rightly pointed out:

> ***"Mahatma Gandhi embodied in his life certain universal principles that are inherent in the moral structure of the universe. These principles are as inescapable as the law of gravitation."***[39]

Those who wish for success in resolving conflict through the Gandhian way, they first of all need courage. Along with this, instead of compulsion, they by accepting the reality, need establish atmosphere of trust and mutual respect.[40]

Further, for resolution, the Gandhian way can be taken in the following two situations:

First: situation when the conflict is over for the time being, or it is continued at any level or in any walk of life, and involved parties wish or long for a resolution, or a resolution becomes necessary, not due to compulsion, but for the lager interest of people.

For this, along with mutual respect and trust, putting down prejudices is also necessary to bring the process in order. Prejudices, in fact, reflect intolerance and insincerity; therefore, they emerge as main obstacles in the solution process. It has no room in the Gandhian way. Thus, after bringing the process in order the following formula comprising of certain points can be adopted for resolution:

- To understand the ground reality of clash, conflict or dispute and that too in current perspective;
- To show sincerity and readiness, and stepping forward to resolution with firm determination; and
- To be ready to sacrifice[41] as the spirit of sacrifice encompasses the knowing of the wellbeing of self to be as important as the wellbeing of humanity as a whole. Making sacrifice in this manner is, in fact, necessary for conducting the universal order in a graceful manner. This spirit of grace stimulates the personal sense of responsibility; it makes the courage of the individual firm. Sacrifice must be understood as the basic attitude of providing the right attention to matters of the larger community in the scope of conflict resolving and of the implementation of harmony. That is why; it not only becomes an essential part of the *Ahimsa*-based Gandhian way, but also emerges as one of the prime points at the time of resolving conflict through this.[42]

In all disputes, clashes or conflicts in general and in those connected with religious sentiments and related to cultural difference in particular, it is necessary that none of the disputant parties feels defeated during the course of resolution process, or even after arriving at a settlement through this method. The *Ahimsa*-based Gandhian way essentially wishes for a win-win situation to all. Therefore, it stresses on working accordingly.

Second: this situation relates to the establishment of justice, or to an urge for equality and freedom. In this regard, having the Gandhian method and also actions taken on the basis of non-violence by the Mahatma himself and others in the centre, a brief discussion has already been attempted. The method established by Gandhi remains intact even today; this seems fully capable in political sphere in particular, but condition is that it should be applied in refined form as per the demand of time and space.

In current perspective the Gandhian way of *Satyagraha* is as unique, effective and adaptable as it was in Gandhi's own lifetime or during the non-violent actions taken by the Afro-Americans in the United States in the second half of the Twentieth Century for the establishment of justice and equality. Its application will remain so in times to come not only in the global perspective, but in the universal context. But, condition remains the same, it must be taken in its refined form and as per the demand of space and time.

Along with this, justness of cause, fair intent, and commitment to *Ahimsa* are also required. The spirit of larger welfare of people should be there in the root of the cause. Under able leadership, strategy, which in fact is an art for ascertaining success, occupies an important place in this universal Gandhian way. But, in this too the condition is that any strategy should not be planned with the intention of defeating the opponent, but winning him and that too with the sole purpose of achieving justice. For this, it must be borne in mind that the opponent –in conflict or dispute, is an opponent until it is afraid of loss, which is again a subject related to mentality. Therefore, as soon as possible the state of fear must be eliminated. The opponent is also an inseparable part of one and the same human family; he has the equal right to exist and rise. Despite the ideological differences his role and contribution in the establishment of harmony is evident and less than none.

Therefore, it is now perhaps most significant to develop understanding in this very perspective not only at national level, but at the global levels, realizing the principle of universal law of balance, harmony and unity. By this, the unnecessary inner human conflict could cease to pave the way for settling external disputes, conflicts and struggles.

As a supreme being, it is the sole responsibility of man to realize and work for the unity of all that live. Man's inner consciousness time and again, or continuously, calls for it. As members of one human family we are capable of resolving conflicts or disputes on the basis of balance, cooperation and harmony –all the three facets of *Ahimsa*, and, thus, in bringing all within the fold of unity. Now, it is high time that we, by spreading this understanding at all levels and in all walks of life, step forward. This act is, in fact, the refinement of the Gandhian concept in current perspective on the one hand and befitting to the very expectation of the universal law from us on the other. Moreover, now it is the time to celebrate the recognition of our inheritance as true universal citizen in our galaxy and to show proudly who we are!

References:

1. Along with cooperation.
2. Bhishma [Devavrata], affectionately called *Bhishma Pitamah*, the eighth son of *Kuru* King Shantanu, said to be blessed with wish-long life, had sworn to serve the ruling Kuru king, was known for his bravery, skill and talent. In one of his instructions to Yudhishthira –the eldest of the *Pandavas*, Bhishma had said that conflict was due to *Adharma*.
3. Vishnugupta Chanakya, Kautilya [370-283 BC], author of the *Arthashastra*, an ancient Indian political treatise, and the founder of the Mauryan Empire in India, clearly advised the rulers for equal treatment and avoid personal gains as inequality and self-interest create the state of conflict and struggle in society.
4. Aristotle [384-322 BC] –the Greek philosopher, in his work entitled, *Poetics*, focused the state of conflict as clash due to opposite principles.
5. Thomas Aquinas [1225-1274] was of the view that wishing glorification was the source of conflict in society.
6. Machiavelli [1469, May 3-1527, June 21] –an Italian statesmen and thinker spoke about conflicts originated of politics.
7. Georg Wilhelm Friedrich Hegel [1770, August 27-1831, November 14] –a German thinker, categorically declared inequalities and economic interest of a particular class of people to be the main cause of social conflicts.

8. Karl Marx [1818, May 5-1883, March 14] –a German sociologist, economist and philosopher, like Hegel, believed that inequality and class interests were the major sources of conflicts –the clash and struggle in society.

9. Ludwing Gumplowicz [1838-1909] –an eminent Polish jurist and political scientist, is recognized as one of the founders of the European sociology.

10. Laster Frank Ward [1841-1913] –a renowned American botanist, paleontologist and sociologist, who became the first chairman of the American Sociological Association.

11. Young India, January 2, 1930

12. Like that of the Greco-Persian War that was fought for a period fifty-one years [499-448 BC] between the City States of Greece and Persians, or the Peloponnesian War for 27 years [431-404 BC] between the City States of Athens and Peloponnesian League [including the City States of Sparta].

13. Like that of the war between England and France fought for a period of 116 years [1337-1553 AD].

14. For example the case related to the War of Kalinga [265-64 BC], fought between Emperor Ashoka and the State of Kalinga –a republic on the coast of present-day Orissa province of India, which ultimately prompted Ashoka to realize and adopt Buddhism, and the American-Vietnamese armed conflict for approximately nineteen years between 1956 and 1976

15. Harijan, April 30, 1938

16. Young India, January 20, 1927

17. Gandhian Thought: New World, New Dimensions, page 34

18. During the course of Non-Cooperation it was on February 5, 1922 that an armed police party fired at the demonstration of *Satyagrahis* at Chauri-Chaura –a place then in the District of

Gorakhpur [now Deoria] of the United Provinces [now Uttar Pradesh]. But when all the bullets were exhausted the police party went inside the police station and bolted themselves in, some of the demonstrators, who were ready to take the course of violence, set the station on fire in which twenty-two police men were killed. Gandhi's soul felt tormented and he asked his compatriots to stop everything.

19. From Champaran to Quit India Movement, page 59 [People like Jawaharlal Nehru, Vallabhbhai Patel and Abul Kalam Azad on the other hand were of the opinion that if the English assured freedom to India after the War, then on this condition, India should help them].

20. Theory and Practice of Gandhian Non-Violence, page 3

21. In this regard clarifying his viewpoint Mahatma Gandhi wrote in Harijan Sewak [Hindi] on August 11, 1940, ***"To cause pain or wish ill to or to take the life of any living being out of a danger or a selfish intent is Himsa. On the other hand after a calm and clean judgment to kill or cause pain to living being with a view to its spiritual or physical benefit from a pure, selfless intent may be the purest form of Ahimsa. Each such case must be judged individually and on its own merits. The final test as its violence or non-violence is after all the intent underlying the act."*** It categorically reveals that non-violence is epitomed in having a tendency and pursuement towards spiritual and/or physical benefit unto everyone without selfishness and with pure thought after cool and clear deliberation. [Essays on Gandhism and Peace, page 23].

22. It is also an eternal value. None of the thinkers-philosophers of repute from any period –ancient to present, great man or religious leader has been unaffected by *Ahimsa*. Also, as the basic source of morality, it occupies its due place in the basics of all religious-communities and preaching-teachings

of their propounders. In this regard, Mahatma Gandhi has rightly pointed out on October 20, 1927 in *Young India*, ***"Non-violence is common to all religions."***

23. *Young India*, March 2, 1922

24. Morality, fully imbued with the spirit of *Ahimsa* is undoubtedly the foremost subject related to man's life to accord strength and to make it meaningful. Further, morality is the fundamental of the *Karma-Phala* theory; not only in *Vedic*-Hinduism, Jainism, Buddhism and Sikhism –the four main religious philosophies of the Indian origin, but in the basics of all other religious philosophies of world also morality occupies the foremost place. It firmly seems becoming the basis of all of them in one way or the other. In all of them *karmas* that are imbued with morality or within the scope of the moral law are regarded as righteous, religious or *dharmik* and those out of its domain are considered as wrong, unrighteous or *adharmik*. In brief, the whole theory of the *Karma-Phala* is based upon moral law and moral values, which is the vital in comparison to others in man's life. Not only this, accepting moral law as the supreme among all the laws, a moral structure at the universal level is considered and declared to be necessary to govern it rightly and properly. The fall or the rise of man depends upon neglecting-discarding or accepting-following-upbringing the moral law, moral values –morality. Those who accepting the moral law in life follow it in their routines or practices, they become capable of making their own life prosperous on the one hand and only they can contribute to the wellbeing of others – humanity as a whole, on the other, and not those who indulge in immoral acts –immorality.

25. Personally, I am of the firm opinion that besides this planet, the earth, there is the life on other planets of the universe also. Man's existence is there. I also believe that the manner science and technologies are growing unprecedentedly; new

dimensions, one after the other, are being added in these spheres and resultantly the world is shrinking rapidly, the day is coming nearer when man's taking the task pertaining to search of life on other planets of the universe will meet to perfection.

26. Accepting the reality that society is not deprived of people ready to support the cause for justice, therefore, the truth.

27. Here one thing should be borne in mind clearly: in the Gandhian way there are always possibilities of compromise at any stage even if partial success is there as it could pave the way for the restoration of justice completely.

28. The above condition applies here also.

29. The spirit in the root of adopting *Swadeshi* was to strengthen the feeling of nationalism in compatriots on the one hand and on the other to make them realized of their self-sufficiency through it.

30. Who formed the organization namely *Khudai Kidmatgar* [servants of God], also known as the *Surkh Posh* [Red Shirt] during twenties of the Twentieth Century, with 1, 00, 000 of its active members to fight through the non-violent Gandhian way, which through the method of strikes, resistance, opposition and boycott achieved success, dominated the politics of the Khyber-Pakhtunkhwa region of the NWFP, now in Pakistan.

31. Particularly in the *Vaikom Satyagraha* under the leadership of TK Madhavan, or in the temple entry movement along with him and people like EV Ramaswami Naicker in the thirties of the Twentieth Century; in the *Vedaranyam Salt Satyagraha* at the time of Civil Disobedience Movement launched by Mahatma Gandhi in 1930.

32. As in Bardoli, under the leadership of Vallabhbhai Patel in the year 1928, or on some of the occasions in peasants'

movements in Oudh or the U. P., which were guided by Jawaharlal Nehru in the second and third decades of the Twentieth Century, respectively.

33. Gandhian Thought: New World, New Dimensions, page 56 [In this regard, Albert Einstein had further added, ***"We should strive to do things in his spirit: not to use violence in fighting for our cause, but by non-participation in anything you believe is evil"].***

34. Ibid.

35. Known as a national icon of the modern American history.

36. Recognized as the first lady of civil rights and the mother of the freedom movement in the US.

37. The leader of the Poor People's Campaign, who also led the March on Washington in 1968

38. One among the most influential and prominent leaders of the *Movement for Civil Rights* in the USA; the director of the *Direct Action and Non-violent Education*, who brought the three known non-violent agitation to success namely: the *Birmingham Children Crusade* [1963]; the *Selma Voting Right Movement* [1965]; and the *Chicago Open Housing Movement* [1966].

39. Non-Cooperation, pp 17-8

40. In this regard, Mahatma Gandhi wrote on April 20, 1940 in the *Harijan*, ***"An atmosphere of mutual respect and trust has to be established as the preliminary step. There can then be no violent conflict between...the masses."***

41. Global Peace, 9/2

42. The root of this point pertaining to sacrifice could be traced in the prime message of the *Bhagavad-Gita*, which influenced Gandhi's life, views and work to the maximum.

Bibliography:

- Gandhi, MK [ed.]. 1933-48. *Harijan Weekly*. Ahmedabad [India]: Harijan Sewak Sangh and Navajivan Trust.
- Gandhi, MK [ed.]. 1919-31. *Young India Weekly*. [reprinted in 1984 in thirteen volumes]. Ahmedabad [India]: Navajivan Trust.
- Kumar, Ravindra. 2002. *From Champaran to Quit India Movement*. New Delhi [India]: Mittal Publications.
- Kumar, Ravindra. 2008. *Gandhian Thought: New World, New Dimensions*. New Delhi [India]: Kalpaz Publications.
- Kumar, Ravindra [ed.]. 2006-11. *Global Peace –International Journal of Philosophy, Peace, Education, Culture and Civilization* [Volume-6, Number-1, September; Volume-7, Numbers-1, 2 and 3, September, December and March; Volume-9, Numbers-2 and 4, December and June; and Volume-10, Numbers -1 and 3, September and March]. Meerut [India]: World Peace Movement Trust.
- Kumar, Ravindra. 2009-10. *India and Mahatma Gandhi* [Hindi and English]. New Delhi [India]: Kalpaz Publications.
- Kumar, Ravindra. 2009. *Non-Cooperation*. Meerut [India]: World Peace Movement Trust.
- Kumar, Ravindra. 2002. *Theory and Practice of Gandhian Non-Violence*. New Delhi [India]: Mittal Publications.
- Kumar, Ravindra. 2001-2. *Towards Peace* [Shanti Ki Aur-Two Volumes in Hindi]. Meerut [India]: Love & Company.
- Rummel, RJ. 1981. *Understanding Conflict and War* [Volumes 5]. California [USA]: Sage Publications

*****

8

Ideal Religiousness of Gandhi: An Analysis

"All that I can, in true humility, present to you is that truth is not to be found by anybody who has not got an abundant sense of humility. If you would swim on the bosom of the ocean of Truth you must reduce yourself to a zero. Further than this I cannot go along this fascinating path."

-MK Gandhi

Introduction

Mahatma Gandhi was a true religious man. He was well acquainted to the fundamentals of all religions of the world. It had developed in him a knowing, an acceptance of esoteric principles of all of them. Furthermore, he had stern faith in God and believed that all religions lead on one pathway to God; God rules the actions of everyone and not a single blade of grass can grow or move without His will. As a constant seeker he said that his faith helped him discover new truths every day. Besides Gopal Krishna Gokhale and Raychandbhai by their living contact, Tolstoy and Ruskin by their works *The Kingdom of God is within you* and *Unto This Last* respectively, Gandhi was deeply impressed by the *Ramacharitmanas* of Tulsidas, the *Gita* and the Bible. Particularly, the teachings of the *Gita* filled in him with the basis of his religious beliefs. In the *Gita*, Lord Krishna, urges Arjuna to dispel doubts about his action against his own kin in the battle for justice. It was the call of duty in his life to perform the duties of a warrior. Krishna's message, that a man must not let distractions divert him from seeking the truth in relation to the development of situation, and thereby realize God, had a profound religious and meaningful effect on him. He was of the opinion that the *Gita* offered salvation through selfless action. Hence, Gandhi's philosophy about duty and service combined with social justice coincided with this aspect of Hinduism that made him an ardent social activist with religious justifications.

Through his addresses and writings, Gandhi inspired to look deep within our hearts to find our true selves. Therefore, his religious thoughts, aspects and application of his religiousness could sum up as follows:

Truth and Non-Violence

Throughout his life Gandhi followed the path of truth and non-violence. He considered truth as God and non-violence an attribute of the soul and stressed on their essential realization in all walk of life. For him, complete faith in truth *Satya* and *Ahimsa* was like a spiritual guide on the pathway to spiritual progress. He insisted that everyone could apply the values of love, truth and non-violence to politics, business or industry just as in private life. He believed if everyone followed truth and non-violence, God would endow with requisite intellect to solve problems. For him God was Supreme and mysterious power that could not be seen but felt; God is everywhere, in everything and His presence can be felt deep within one's heart.

He said:

"There is an indefinable mysterious power that pervades everything. I feel it, though I do not see it. It is this unseen power that makes it felt and yet defies proof, because it is so unlike all that I perceive through my senses. It transcends reason. But it is possible to reason out the existence of God to a limited extent."[1]

Realization of Truth

Gandhi was aware of the complexity of life and of the fact that the development of human mind is not the same for everyone. Hence, the perception of truth might be different for different people. Still truth is truth and it cannot be changed. Just like many people reason the existence of God, though He is unseen, still His existence can be felt by heart. He knew that while leading a life with high values of *Satya* and *Ahimsa*, there could be problems. So, he stressed on applying patient and constant efforts in the right direction to realize truth and emphasized on offering silent prayers to help one continue on the right path. God can be realized in truth, love, ethics and morality. That God is the source of spiritual light and life on earth, and still beyond the reach of intellect. In his own words:

"All that I can, in true humility, present to you is that truth is not to be found by anybody who has not got an abundant sense of humility. If you would swim on the bosom of the ocean of Truth you must reduce yourself to a zero. Further than this I cannot go along this fascinating path."[2]

God: Truth and Love

Since his young age, Gandhi used to recite the *Sahastranama* [a thousand names of God] as each name was an attribute in praise of Him. Still deep in his heart he believed that He is the Ultimate Truth. But truth being pure and a means of realizing God, he considered Truth as God. The best way to realize truth was through love in the form of *Ahimsa* and the meaning of *Ahimsa* was not only non-violence but also active care and love for all living beings and thus a means to realize truth.

He admitted:

"I do dimly perceive that whilst everything around me is ever changing, ever dying, there is underlying all that change a living power that is changeless, that holds all together, that creates, dissolves and recreates. That informing power or spirit is God. And since nothing else I see merely through the senses can or will persist, He alone is. And is this power benevolent or malevolent? I see it as purely benevolent, for I can see that in the midst of death life persists, in the midst of untruth truth persists, in the midst of darkness light persists. Hence I gather that God is Life, Truth, Light. He is Love. He is the supreme Good."[3]

Realization of God

For Gandhi God is within everyone. God is an unseen power, but is as near to one as flesh to fingernails. He was of the view that there are some hidden spiritual powers inside each and everyone, which could be discovered by constant and right effort. The Supreme Power i.e. God within oneself can also be realized by fixed determination and stern faith. On the way of developing such faith, the practice of *Ahimsa* is necessary. Moreover, God resides in each and everyone, therefore, all living beings are equal and identical; and to hurt one would be like hurting God Himself. Such thoughts are not only in accordance with the teachings of the *Gita* but also similar to what great Saints like Guru Nanak or Kabir have preached.

To quote the *Gita*:

"I [God] am the sacrifice, the fire, the incense. I am

the father, the mother of this universe; the mystic doctrine, the syllable Om, the Vedas; the path, the support, the master, the witness, the habitation, the refuge, the friend; origin, and dissolution, and inexhaustible seed I am ambrosia, and death; what exists and what exists not; the soul, in the heart of all beings: beginning, middle, and end."[4]

In the words of Guru Nanak:

"God is within you as the perfume is in the flower and the image in the mirror. He is deep down at the bottom of your hearts. There He must be sought."[5]

And Kabir:

"As oil is in sesame seed, and fire is in flint, so the Lord is within you, unrevealed..." and ***"The entire universe has come into being from one Light, Therefore how can one be good and another bad!"***[6]

Faith in Religion

Gandhi's belief remained in the most ancient and original form of Hinduism, which he considered to be a pure faith. There was no idol worship in it and that because of materialism the original form of Hinduism was tainted with some social evils. He also believed that through all ages God has manifested Himself in different forms and has incarnated from time-to-time for helping people on the pathway to salvation. Deeply influenced by the sayings of the *Bhagavadgita*, and particularly by message it conveys he writes:

***"When there is decay of righteousness and there is exaltation of unrighteousness, then I [God] myself come forth. For the protection of the good, for the destruction of the evildoers, for the sake of firmly establishing righteousness, I am born from age to age."*[7]**

Gandhi considered him to be a poor soul caught in struggle and yearning to be all good, fully truthful and completely non-violent in thoughts, words and deed. Such an approach was often painful yet he never gave up his faith and with each difficulty he grew stronger, prepared for the next challenge with utmost humility. In his life story he admits:

***"But the path of self-purification is hard and steep; to attain to perfect purity one has to become absolutely passion-free in thought, speech and action; to rise above the opposing currents of love and hatred, attachment and repulsion."*[8]**

Self-surrender

Since childhood, humans are taught to approach life dynamically. Everyone in this world wishes to better his prospects and make mark in his respective field of action. If there is an instance of injustice, people tend to assert their rights and privileges. Some do it the right way and some choose the wrong way. But throughout his life, Gandhi remained a seeker of truth, which could be realized by self-effacement. He called it surrendering oneself and 'making oneself a zero' before the Supreme. To quote from his autobiography again:

"But I know that I have still before me a difficult path to traverse. I must reduce myself to zero. So long

as one does not of his own free will put himself last among his fellow creatures, there is no salvation for him."[9]

Man's egotism makes him falsely believe of his superiority over his fellow creatures. While after some reflection, the vanity of the mortal frame can easily be felt. Man's life is like a bubble, is short and end is certain so what's dignified in it. That is why; Gandhi believes that if we realize our oneness with the Eternal, we can share the same dignity just like when a drop of ocean is separated from it, it has no worth, but if it remains with the ocean, it is ocean itself. In this regard his views were in harmony to many saints and sages. To quote Guru Nanak:

"***Wealth, youth and flowers last for a short time; like the Pabban*** [a small flowering plant] ***leaves; they wither away as they sprout."*** And to Kabir, ***"You are no more than a bubble, so transitory; you will disappear in the moment of an eye, as the morning start vanishes; even while you gaze at it."***[10]

Self-restraint

Human mind is a constant wanderer; try to apply it on one thing and it runs to another. As such it has always been difficult to concentrate. Gandhi was aware of this fact. But being a true seeker, he never gave up on finding a way out. Through his deep religious knowledge, he came to the conclusion that self-restraint was essential not only for spiritual progress, but also for the realization of *Satya* and *Ahimsa*. Too much physical harmony and comfort could hinder a person to develop humility and create obstacles on the pathway to realize

God. Hence, he said that all physical and intellectual energies should be concentrated on God and serving of humanity. For this purpose, he stressed the practice of self-restraint and set some rules in regards of various actions.

Food

The Mahatma believed, what a man eats affects his temperament. Man's passion is generally co-existent with a longing for the pleasures of the palate. Even milk stimulated animal passion and in 1912, therefore, Gandhi completely abstained himself of milk and recommended use of seasonal fruits and nuts that are considered nourishing to the nerves and tissues. Gandhi advised that the one, who wished to realize God, should change his food habits and stressed the practice of self-restraint in food habits, going from simple food to simplest. To quote him:

"One should eat not in order to please the palate but just to keep the body going. When each organ or sense sub-serves the body and through the body the soul, its specific relish disappears, and then alone does it begin to function in the way nature intended it to do. Any number of experiments is too small and no sacrifice is too great for attaining this symphony with nature."[11]

Fast

Gandhi believed that mind is at the root of all senses. It is only the control of mind that can bring control over all senses, essential for one's spiritual growth. Therefore, fasting is very useful in this regard. For, Gandhi writes in Young India:

"It is my firm belief that the strength of the soul grows in proportion as you subdue the flesh."[12]

He warned that fasting should not be accompanied by thoughts of delicacies, which one might wish to consume after completion of the fast. Such a fasting could neither help in restraining food habits nor desire. The fasting must come from the depth of one's soul and should be done with patience, single-mindedness and perfect calm.

Continence

Gandhi believed in practicing self-control in domestic life as well as in thought and speech. He also believed that the victory over lust is the highest achievement of a person's existence. Without winning over one's lust, there could be no hope of getting full control over oneself and without that, there could be no *Swarajya* or *Ramarajya*. The noble things like serving the downtrodden, developing communal harmony, *Khadi*, cow-protection and village development were not possible without a great deal of spiritual strength, which in turn could only be gained by God's grace. And that God's grace could not be bestowed on someone already a slave of lust. In his autobiography he writes:

"I think it is the height of ignorance to believe that the sexual act is an independent function necessary like sleeping or eating. The world depends for its existence on the act of generation, and as the world is the playground of God and a reflection of His glory, the act of generation should be controlled for the ordered growth of the world. He who realizes this will control his lust

at any cost, equip himself with the knowledge necessary for the physical, mental and spiritual well-being of his progeny, and give the benefit of that knowledge to posterity."[13]

Gandhi considered continence to be difficult to practice. He said that mind was even hard to control than wind, but the stern faith in God, Who resides in everyone's heart, could make it possible. He advised to non-cooperate one's mind in its evil and lustful wanderings. He believed that victory over self could be gained in this manner.

Non-possession

The *Gita* was the scripture that inspired Gandhi for non-possession. He believed that people wishing for spiritual growth and desired salvation should give up their attachments to the things they own. They should act like trustees. They should never consider them the owner of the things in their possession. This philosophy and understanding brought a great change in Mahatma Gandhi and he began to apply it in a wider sense. Speaking in Madras on February 2, 1916 he said:

"I suggest that we are thieves in a way. If I take anything that I do not need for my own immediate use, and keep it, I thieve it from somebody else. I venture to suggest that it is the fundamental law of Nature, without exception, that Nature produces enough for our wants from day to day, and if only everybody took enough for himself and nothing more, there would be no pauperism in this world, there would be no man dying of starvation in this world."[14]

Serving Humanity, Serving God

Gandhi is known for his service to humanity. He had a passion for serving the needy, neglected and downtrodden. Whenever the situation demanded, he used to give up his work and not only engaged himself, but his whole household in serving humanity. He derived pleasure from it; considered it like discharging a debt. The joy he gained from it was just similar to the one, which is felt on the lightening of a burden. He believed in oneness of God; everyone is equal before God; God resides in each and every heart, so he considered service to humanity as essential for the ultimate realization of God. In this regard he writes:

"The immediate service of all human beings becomes a necessary part of the endeavours, simply because the only way to find God is to see Him in His creation and be one with it."[15]

Religious Tolerance

As all religions lead to the same ultimate goal of the realization of God, therefore, Gandhi stressed the development of religious tolerance. He was of the view that the esoteric principles of all religions are the same; the Hindu philosophy sees all as consisting of the elements of truth, hence developing a sense of respect and reverence towards all. He considered different religions as branches of one tree and stressed on the need of study of all of them. He even advocated for the inclusion of the study of other religions in school curriculum. He called upon his countrymen:

"A curriculum of religious instruction should include a study of the tenets of faiths other than one's own. For this purpose the students should be trained to cultivate the habit of understanding and appreciating the doctrines of various great religions of the world in a spirit of reverence and broad-minded tolerance."[16]

Fearlessness

During the course of Indian freedom movement, Gandhi traveled across the country and during his travels he noticed that the people of India lived in fear. People had their opinions in regards of religious, social and political changes, but did not speak about them in public. In this regard, Mahatma Gandhi called upon the people to become fearless. He said that God is one. God is the only True Ruler and above all; therefore, give up all fear. A person, who fears God and has stern faith in Him, cannot fear anything on earth. Gandhi considered *Ahimsa* to be a form of highest love and a great service towards humanity. He stressed on developing the love even for enemy, an inimical wrongdoer, a wrong doing stranger and a wrong doing relative. Such an approach requires truth and fearlessness on the part of a person but to develop total fearlessness, one has to cultivate that capacity of sacrifice. He clarified:

"Non-violence in its dynamic condition means conscious suffering. It does not mean meek submission to the will of the evil-doer, but it means the putting of one's whole soul against the will of the tyrant."[17]

He also said:

> ***"He who has not overcome all fear cannot practice Ahimsa to perfection. The votary of Ahimsa has only one fear that is of God. He who seeks refuge in God ought to have a glimpse of the Atman*** [Soul] ***that transcends the body; and the moment one has a glimpse of the Imperishable Atman one sheds the love of the perishable body."***[18]

Prayer

Gandhi considered praying to be the essence of religion and it should be the centre of one's spiritual life as without prayer from the heart, true faith could not be developed. And that prayer expresses a soul's longing. Hence, Gandhi shunned the use of mechanical prayers and callous chants and stressed that prayer should not be an act of show. He insisted that prayer should not be bound by words but should come straight from the heart, because only in this manner it will be able to cleanse the passions from the heart and make one feel close to God. He was clearly of the opinion:

> ***"My religion teaches me that whenever there is distress, which one cannot remove, one must fast and pray."*** And, ***"One discovers truth and the method of applying the only legitimate means of vindicating it i.e., Satyagraha or soul-force, by patient endeavour and silent prayer."***[19]

Vegetarianism

In Gandhi's time it was said that vegetarianism had made

Indians weak in mind and body and passive in action. He denounced this thought and considered vegetarianism the priceless gift. He himself was a strict follower of vegetarianism and believed that non-vegetarian food was not suitable for human beings and they have erred in copying such food habits from carnivorous animals. In India's case for *Swarajya* he writes:

"I do feel that spiritual progress does demand at some stage that we should cease to kill our fellow creatures for the satisfaction of our bodily wants."[20]

His love for vegetarianism was shown when his wife had undergone an operation in Durban and was very weak. She was under the care of a doctor while Gandhi was away for some time. The doctor wanted to prescribe some non-vegetarian diet, but both of them were not agree without caring the life at stake. She was taken to Phoenix settlement at once and put under hydropathic treatment after which she gained strength.

Religion and Politics

For Gandhi politics was a means to bring good to all. He believed that religion inspired politics is capable of bringing social change in the masses. In order to realize the universal spirit of truth there is a need to develop love and compassion towards every living being. To him every human being was equal irrespective of caste, creed or social status. In his autobiography he said:

"That is why my devotion to truth has drawn me

into the field of politics; and I can say without the slightest hesitation, and yet in all humility, that those who say that religion has nothing to do with politics, they do not know what religion means.”[21]

He clarified further:

“My work of social reform was in no way less or subordinate to political work. The fact is, that when I saw that to a certain extent my social work would be impossible without the help of political work, I took to the latter and only to the extent that it helped the former. I must therefore confess that work of social reform or self-purification of this nature is a hundred times dearer to me than what is called purely political work.”[22]

Concept of *Ramarajya*

Mahatma Gandhi was deeply devoted to the *Ramayana*, the story of Rama, the ideal king. This epic establishes the ideal morals that can ever be experienced in human life. It sets the standards for the value of one's promise, the utmost respect of children for their parents, true sacrifice, ideal character, selfless living, ideal governance and at last victory of good over evil. Gandhi regarded it as one of the greatest religious books and wished to establish an ideal state based on its values. He dreamt of a state in which there would be no government and where each and every one would be governed by himself in such a manner that there could be no grievances caused to anyone. In such a manner there would be a state of perfect harmony and peace. He named it the *Ramarajya*. Addressing the people of Bhavnagar on January 8, 1925, he said:

"My Ideal of Indian States is that of Ramarajya. Rama taking his cue from a washer man's remark and in order to satisfy his subjects abandoned Sita who was dear to him as life itself and was a very incarnation of Purity. Rama did justice even to a dog. By abandoning his kingdom and living in the forest for the sake of truth Rama gave to all the kings of the world an object lesson in noble conduct. By his strict monogamy he showed that a royal householder could lead a life of perfect self-restraint. He lent splendour to his throne by his popular administration and proved that Ramarajya was the acme of Swarajya. Rama did not need the very imperfect modern instrument of ascertaining public opinion by counting votes. He had captivated the hearts of the people. He knew public opinion by intuition as it were. The subjects of Rama were supremely happy."[23]

Conclusion

As such, apart from the socio-political achievements of Mahatma Gandhi, he is well remembered as a great religious reformer. He was not only one of the chief architects of Indian independence but also a reformer of Hinduism. He was a Hindu, but also a critic of some practices of traditional Hinduism. He once said:

"Let me explain what I mean by religion. It is not the Hindu religion which I certainly prize above all other religions, but the religion which transcends Hinduism, which changes one's very nature, which binds one indissolubly to the truth within and which ever purifies."[24]

Gandhi is also remembered for his trust in women's moral and spiritual strength. He considered women as an important part of the Indian Freedom Movement. He called upon the women to be brave and inspired them to cast off their image of ***"dolls and objects of indulgence."*** He asked them to act as comrades on their husband's side. All his life he also fought against the practice of untouchability, considered it unjustified and a blot on the face of Hinduism. He started calling the untouchables as Harijan, ***"People of God."***

More than six decades have passed since the sad and unfortunate demise of the Mahatma, but today the need to learn and apply his thoughts is much more than ever by all in general and particularly Asians. Gandhi's ideal noble thoughts call upon us to step forward on the pathway to truth and non-violence to achieve perfect harmony and above all spiritual realization.

References:

1. Young India, October 11, 1928
2. Ibid, December 31, 1931
3. Ibid, October 11, 1928
4. Global Peace International Journal, 9/1
5. Ibid
6. Ibid
7. Ibid
8. Ibid
9. Ibid
10. Ibid

11. Ibid.

12. Young India, October 2, 1924

13. Global Peace International Journal, 9/1

14. Ibid

15. Harijan, August 29, 1936

16. Young India, December 6, 1928

17. Ibid, August 11, 1920

18. Harijan, September 1, 1940

19. Young India, June 1, 1921

20. Global Peace International Journal 9/1

21. Ibid

22. Young India, August 6, 1931

23. Global Peace International Journal, 9/1

24. Young India, May 12, 1920 [Recognizing the importance of Gandhi's views on the subject even in current perspective the whole text of his write up is given in the Appendix–2].

Bibliography:

- CBT. 1989. *Remembering Our Leaders*. New Delhi [India]: Children's Book Trust.

- Deogirikar, TR. 1992. [Forth edition]. *Gopal Krishna Gokhale.* New Delhi [India]: Publications Division, Ministry of Information and Broadcasting, Government of India.

- Gandhi, MK [ed.]. 1936-40. *Harijan Weekly*. Ahmedabad [India]: Harijan Sewak Sangh and Navajivan Trust.

- Gandhi, MK [ed.]. 1919-31. *Young India Weekly*. [Reprinted in 13 Volumes in 1984]. Ahmedabad [India]: Navajivan Publishing House.

- Kumar, Ravindra [ed.]. 2009. *Global Peace –International Journal of Philosophy, Peace, Education, Culture and Civilization* [Volume-9, Number-1, Supplementary]

*****

Appendices

"Bluster is no religion nor is vast learning stored in capacious brains. The seat of religion is in the heart. We Hindus, Christians, Musalmans and others have to write the interpretation of our respective faiths with our own crimson blood and not otherwise."

-MK Gandhi

1
A Candid Critic

"I must not withhold the following letter[1] from the readers:

'I have perused your article *Swamiji the Martyr*[2] with the care and reverence it deserves. I have read it five times before attempting to criticize it. This is to avoid hasty criticism. The article is undoubtedly written in fascinating language. I envy your style, it attracts, but to me it appears, that it is rather dangerously attractive. My criticism is based on my estimation of your character. I have often debated with some friends on this subject. They hold that you are a statesman in the garb of a saint –ready to forgo truth in the cause of your country. I have on the contrary maintained that you are a saint –who has entered politics in fulfillment of your mission, to practice truth in the face of most trying and perplexing circumstances. I shall be very obliged to know if my estimation is correct. For if it is not, the criticism that follows has little value. I am of the opinion that a man of policy it is his rights to write in the manner you have done.

'You will agree with me that to suppress truth is a form of falsehood; to refuse to call a spade when you feel it like that is cowardice and that fearlessness and truth go together. Do you feel, Mahatmaji, that the murder of Swamiji was an inhuman, barbarous and cruel act of a Muslim ruffian and that the entire Muslim community should be ashamed of it? Why do you refuse to characterize it as such? Instead of condemning the deed and the doer, and those who are responsible for this act [those who describe Hindu leaders as *Kafirs* –the hot Muslim propagandists and the mad Muslim priests], you have begun to defend the murderer and hold an apology for the community. You never defended Dyer. Is not a European a brother too?

'You say further, Islam means peace. Is this truth? Islam as taught by Quran and practiced by Muslims ever since its birth never meant peace. What makes you write a thing so patently wrong? Buddhism, Christianity, and Hinduism of course teach peace, but not Islam. May I know what makes you think and write like this?

'You never minced matters when condemning the wrong of the Government, you never minced matters when you condemned *Arya Samaj*, why fear to condemn Muslims for even proved wrongs! I am sure if such a black act had been committed by a Hindu against a Muslim leader [which Heaven forbid!], you would have condemned the murderer and the community in unsparing terms. You would have asked Hindus to repent in sack-cloth and ashes, to offer fasts, hold *hartal*, raise memorial to the departed Muslim and many other things. Why do you accord preferential treatment to your *blood brothers* –the Muslims? A truth-teller knows no fear, not even of the sword of Islam and I trust you will oblige me by giving reply to above in the columns of your esteemed weekly.'

"The writer is frank and obviously in earnest and reflects the prevalent mood.

"To clothe me with sainthood is too early even if it is

possible. I myself do not feel a saint in any shape or form. But I do feel I am a votary of Truth in spite of all my errors of unconscious omission and commission. The correspondent has judged rightly that I am not *a statesman in the grab of a saint*. But since Truth is the highest wisdom, sometimes my acts appear to be consistent with the highest statesmanship. But I hope I have no policy in me save the policy of truth and *ahimsa*. I will not sacrifice truth and *ahimsa* even for the deliverance of my country or religion. This is as much as to say that neither can be delivered.

"In writing about the assassination of Swamiji, I have not surpassed truth. I do believe the act to be all that the correspondent describes. But I feel pity for the murderer even as I felt for General Dyer. Let not the correspondent forget that I refused to be party to any agitation for the prosecution of General Dyer. I do claim that a European is just as much brother to me as a Musalman Indian or a Hindu.

"When I do feel about the assassin is that he is himself a victim of foul irreligious propaganda in the name of religion. Hence it is that I have held the newspapers that have corrupted the public mind to be responsible for the murder. I do hold the *maulvis* and all those who have indulged in exciting hatred against Swamiji to be responsible.

"But I do regard Islam be a religion of peace in the same sense as Christianity, Buddhism and Hinduism are. No doubt there are differences in degree but the object of these religions is peace. I know the passages that can be quoted from the Quran to the contrary. But so is it possible to quote passages from the *Vedas* to the contrary. What is the meaning of imprecations pronounced against the *Anaryas*? Of course these passages bear today a different meaning but at one time they did wear a dreadful aspect. What is the meaning of the treatment of untouchables by us Hindus? Let not the pot call kettle. The fact is that we are all growing. I have given my opinion that the followers of Islam are too free with the sword. But that is not due to the teaching of the Quran. That is due to in my opinion to the environment in which Islam was born. Christianity has a bloody record against it not because Jesus was found wanting but because the environment in which it spread was not responsive to his lofty teachings.

"These two, Christianity and Islam, are after all religions of but yesterday. They are yet in the course of being interpreted. I reject the claim of *maulvis* to give a final interpretation to the message of Mohammad as I reject that of the Christian clergy to give a final interpretation to the message of Jesus. Both are being interpreted in the lines of those who are living these messages in silence and in perfect self-dedication. Bluster is no religion nor is vast learning stored in capacious brains. The seat of religion is in the heart. We Hindus, Christians, Musalmans and others have to write the interpretation of our respective faiths with our own crimson blood and not otherwise."

2
Neither a Saint nor a Politician

"A kind friend has sent me the following cutting from the April number of the *East and West:*

'Mr. Gandhi has the reputation of a saint but it seems that the politician in him often dominates his decisions. He has been making great use of *hartals* and there can be no gain saying that under his direction *hartal* it becoming a powerful political weapon for uniting the educated and the uneducated on a single question of the day. The *hartal* is not without its disadvantages. It is a teaching direct action, and direct action however potent does not work for unity. Is Mr. Gandhi quite sure that he is serving the highest behests of *ahimsa*, harmlessness? His proposal to commemorate the shooting at Jallianwala Bagh is not likely to promote concord. It is a tragic incident into which our government was betrayed, but is the memory of its bitterness worth retaining? Can we not commemorate the event by raising a temple of peace, to help the widows and orphans to bless the souls of those who died without knowing why? The world is full of politicians and pettifoggers who, in the name of patriotism, poison the inner sweetness of man and, as a result, we have wars and feuds and such shameless slaughter as turned Jallianwala Bagh into a shambles. Shall we not now try for a larger symbiosis such as Buddha and Christ preached, and brings the world to breathe and prosper together? Mr. Gandhi seemed destined to be the apostle of such a movement, but circumstances are forcing him to seek the way of raising resistances and group unities. He may yet take up the larger mission of uniting the world.'

"I have given the whole of the quotation. As a rule I do not notice criticism of me or my methods except when there by I acknowledge a mistake or enforce still further the principles criticized I have a double reason for noticing the extract. For, not only do I hope further to elucidate the principles. I hold dear, but I want to show my regard for the author of the criticism whom I know and whom I have admired for many years for the singular beauty of his character. The critic regrets to see in me a politicians, where as he has expected me to be a saint. Now I think that the world *saint* should be ruled out of present life. It is too sacred a word to be lightly applied to anybody, much less to one like myself who claims only to be a humble searcher after truth, knows his limitations, makes mistakes, never hesitates to admit them when he makes them, and frankly confesses that he, like a scientist, is making experiments about some *'of the eternal varieties'* of life, but cannot even claim to be a scientist because he can show no tangible proof of scientific accuracy in his methods or such tangible results of his experiments as modern science demands. But though a disclaiming sainthood I disappoint the critic's expectations, I would have him to give up his regrets by answering him that the politician in me has never dominated a single decision of mine, and if I seem to take part in politics, it is only because politics encircle us today like the coil of the snake from which one cannot get out, no matter how much one tries. I wish therefore to wrestle with the snake, as I have been doing with more or less success consciously since 1894, unconsciously, as I have now discovered ever since reaching years of discretion. Quite selfishly as I wish to live in peace in the midst of bellowing storm howling round me, I have been experimenting with myself and my friends by introducing religion into politics. Let me explain what I mean by religion. It is not the Hindu religion which I certainly prize above all other religions, but the religion which transcends Hinduism, which changes one's very nature, which blinds one indissolubly to the truth within and with ever purities. It is the permanent element in human nature which counts no cost to great in order to find full expression and which leaves the soul utterly restless until it has found itself, known its maker and appreciated the true correspondence between the Maker and itself.

"It was in that religious spirit that I came upon *hartal*. I wanted to show that it is not knowledge of letters, that would give India consciousness of her, or that would find the educated together. The *hartal* illuminated the whole of India as if by magic on the 6th of April 1919 and had it not been for the interruption of the 10th of April brought about by Satan whispering fear into the ears of a government conscious of its own wrong and inciting to anger a people that were prepared for it by utter distrust of the government, India would have risen to an unimaginable height. The hartal had not only been taken up by the great masses of people in a truly religious spirit but it was intended to be a prelude to a series of direct actions. "But my critic deplores direct action. For, he says, *"it does not work for unity."* I join issue with him. Never has anything been done on this earth without direct action. I rejected the word *passive resistance,* because of its insufficiency and its being interpreted as a weapon of the weak. It was direct action in South Africa which told and told so effectively that it converted

General Smuts to sanity. He was in 1906 the most relentless opponent of Indian aspirations. In 1914 he took pride in doing tardy justice by removing from the statute Book of the Union of disgraceful measure which, in 1909 he had told Lord Morley, would be never removed, for he then said South Africa would never tolerate repeal of a measure which was twice passed by the Transvaal Legislature. But what is more, direct action sustained for eight years left behind not only no bitterness, but the very Indians who put up sue a stubborn fight against General Smuts, ranged themselves round his banner in 1915 and fought under him in East Africa. It was direct action in Champaran which removed an age-1ong grievance. A meek submission when one is chatting under a disability or a grievance which one would gladly see removed, not only does not make for unity, but makes the weak party…angry and prepares him for an opportunity to explode. By allying myself with the weak party by teaching him directly, firm but harmless action, I make him feel strong and capable of defying the physical might. He feels braced for the struggle, regains confidence in him and knowing that the remedy lies with him, ceases to harbor the spirit of revenge and learns to be satisfied with a redress of the wrong he is seeking to remedy.

"It is working along the same line that I have ventured to suggest a memorial about Jallianwala Bagh. The writer in East and West has ascribed to me a proposal which has never once crossed my mind. He thinks I want, *"to commemorate the shooting at Jallianwala Bagh."* Nothing can be further from my thought than to perpetuate the memory of a black deed. I dare say that before we have come to our own, we shall have a repetition of the tragedy and I will prepare the nation for it by treasuring the memory of the innocent dead. The widows and the orphans have been and are being helped but we cannot *"bless the souls of those who died without knowing why"*, if we will not acquire the ground which has been hallowed by innocent blood and there erect a suitable memorial for them. It is not to serve, if I can help it, as a reminder of foul deed but it shall serve as an encouragement to the nation that it is better to die helpless and unarmed and as victims rather than as tyrants. I would have the future generations remember that we who witnessed the innocent dying did not ungratefully refuse to cherish their memory. As Mrs. Jinnah truly remarked when she gave her mite to the fund, the memorial is erected that will decide its character.

"What was the large *'symbioses'* that Buddha and Christ preached? Buddha fearlessly carried the war into the enemy's camp and brought down on its knees an arrogant priesthood. Christ drove out the money-changers from the temple of Jerusalem and drew down curses from Heaven upon the hypocrites and the *pharidees*. Both were for intensely direct action. But even as Buddha and Christ chastised they showed unmistakable gentleness and love behind every act of their. They would not raise a finger against their enemies, but would gladly surrender themselves rather than the truth for which they lived. Buddha would have died resisting the priesthood, if the majesty of his love had not proved to be equal to the task of bending the priesthood. Christ died on the cross with a crown of thorns on his head defying the might of a whole empire. And if I raised resistances of a non-violent character I simply and humbly follow in the footsteps of the great teachers named by my critics.

"Lastly, the writer of the paragraph quarrels with me, *'grouping unites'* and would have me to take up *'the larger mission of uniting the world.'* I once told him under a common roof that I was probably more cosmopolitan than he. I abide by that expression. Unless I group unities I shall never be able to unite the whole world. Tolstoy once said that if we would but let off the backs of our neighbors the world would be quite alright without any further help for us. And if we can only serve our immediate neighbors by ceasing to upon them, the circle of unities thus grouped in the right fashion will never grow in circumference till at last it is conterminous with that of the whole world. More than that it is not given to any man to try or achieve. [यथा पिण्डे तथा ब्रह्माण्डे] is as true today as ages ago when it was first uttered by an unknown *Rishi*."

1. He received from one of his compatriots soon after the murder of Swami Shradhanand.

2. Swami Shradhanand [Note: In his write up entitled, *Swamiji the Martyr*, the Mahatma has pointed out, ***"The expected has happened. Swami Shraddhanandji passed a day or two at the Satyagraha Ashram at Sabarmati, now about six months ago, and told me, in the course of his conversations that he often received letters threatening his life. Where is the reformer who has not a price put upon his head? There was, therefore, nothing untoward to his getting the letters. And there is nothing untoward in the assassination having taken place. Swamiji was a reformer; he was a man of action not of words. His was a living belief. He had suffered for it. He was bravery personified. He never quailed before danger. He was a worrier. And a worrier loves to die, not on a sick-bed, but on the battlefield. Shraddhanandji became seriously ill about a month ago. Dr. Ansari was, as his physician, giving him all the loving attention he was capable of giving. The telegram I***

received from his son, Indra, in reply to my inquiry at the beginning of the month, was that he was better and that he wanted my 'love and prayer' both of which he had before the asking. God had willed for him a martyr's death and so though he was still on the sick-bed, he died at the hands of an assassin who had asked to be admitted to the Swamiji's presence for the purpose of holding a religious discourse on Islam, who was admitted at the Swamiji's instance, and who, under pretence of wanting water to quench his thirst, had Swamiji's faithful servant, Dharam Singh, sent out to fetch water, and who, in absence of the servant, deposited two death wounds in the patient's breast, as he was lying in his bed. We have not the last words of the Swamiji, but if I knew him at all, I have no doubt that he prayed to his God to forgive him who knew not that he was doing anything wrong. In the language of the Gita, therefore, 'happy the worrier who achieves such a blessed death.' Death is at any time blessed, but it is twice blessed for a worrier who dies for his cause, i.e. truth. Death is no fiend; he is the truest of friends. He delivers us from agony. He helps us against ourselves. He ever gives us new chances, new hope. He is like sleep a sweet restorer. Yet it is customary to mourn when a friend dies. The custom has no operation when the death is that of a martyr. I cannot, therefore, mourn over this death. He and his are to be envied. For though Shraddhanandji is dead, he is yet living. He is living in a truer sense than when he moved about in our midst in his giant body. The family in which he was born, the nation to which he belonged are to be congratulated upon so glorious a death as this. He lived a hero. He has died a hero. But there is another side to the shield. I regard myself as a friend of Musalmans. They are my blood brothers. Their wrongs are my wrongs. I share their sorrows and their joys. Any evil deed done by a Musalman hurts me just as much as that done by a Hindu. This foul deed has been done by one who bears a Musalman name. As a friend of the Musalmans, therefore, I deeply regret the event. The joy of the death is thus tempered by the sorrow that an erring, misguided brother has been the cause of it. Martyrdom can, therefore, never be wished for. It becomes a thing of joy only when it comes unsought. We may not gloat over the errors of the least of our fellows. But the fact is that an error often refuses to become patent until it becomes atrocious. It dies only after being completely disgraced. This tragedy has national importance. It draws pointed attention to An evil that is

eating into the vitals of the nation. Both Hindus and Musalmans have the choice before them. We are both on trial. Hindus may, by being resentful, disgrace Hinduism and postpone the unity that must come. They can by self-restraint show themselves to be worthy of the message of Upanishads and of Yudhishthira who was the embodiment of forgiveness. Let us not ascribe the crime of an individual to a whole community. Let us not harbour the spirit of retaliation. Let us not think of the wrong as done by a Musalman against a Hindu, but of an act erring brother against a hero. Musalmans have an ordeal to pass through. There can be no doubt that they are too free with the knife and the pistol. The sword is no emblem of Islam. But Islam was born in an environment where the sword was and still remains the supreme law. The message of Jesus has proved ineffective because the environment was unready to receive it. So with the message of the Prophet. The sword is yet too much in evidence among Musalmans. It must be sheathed if Islam is to be what it means –peace. There is danger of Musalmans secretly endorsing the mad deed. It will be a calamity for them and the world. For ours is after all a world problem. Reliance upon the sword is wholly inconsistent with reliance upon God. There should be, on their part, unequivocal mass condemnation of the atrocity. I wish to plead for Abdul Rashid [the killer of Swamiji]. I do not know who he is. It does not matter to me what prompted the deed. The fault is ours. The newspaper man has become a walking plague. He spreads the contagion of lies and calumnies. He exhausts the foul vocabulary of his dialect, and injects his virus into the unsuspecting, and often receptive minds of his readers. Leaders 'intoxicated with the exuberance of their own language' have not known to put a curb upon their tongue or pens. Secret and insidious propaganda has done its dark and horrible work, unchecked and unabashed. It is therefore we the educated and the semi-educated class, that are responsible for the hot fever with possessed Abdul Rashid. It is unnecessary to discriminate and apportion the blame between the rival parties. Where both are to blame, who can attribute with golden scales and fix the exact ratio of blame? It is no part of self- defence to tell lies or exaggerate. It is too much to hope, but Swamiji was great enough to warrant the hope that his blood may wash us of our guilt, cleans our hearts and cement these two mighty divisions of the human family..."

*****

Who's Who

Ansari, MA	: [1880-1936] was a nationalist, a leader of the Indian National Congress and the Muslim League, both; was also one of the founders of the *Jamia Millia Islamia* of Delhi
Arjuna	: One of the greatest warrior [in Indian mythology] on the earth and the third of the *Pandavas* –the heroes of the Hindu epic *Mahabharata*, who played a key role in the victory of *Pandavas* in the *War of Mahabharata*, was also a close friend of Lord Krishna from whom he heard the *Gita* before the battle of Kurukshetra
Bhave, Vinoba	: [1895, September 11-1982, November 15] popularly known as the *Acharya*, was a leading freedom fighter and was also considered as the spiritual successor of Mahatma Gandhi; became universally

renowned for the *Bhoodan Andolan* after India's freedom.

Gokhale, Gopal Krishna : [1866-1915] was one of the leading social and political leaders of India and a senior Congressman, who founded the *Servant of India Society*, and Mahatma Gandhi declared him to be his political guru

Kabir, the Mahatma : [1398-1518] was a well-known saint in the medieval period from north India, who preached the essential unity of Godhead and harmony among religious communities

Krishna, the Lord : A central figure of Hinduism, traditionally attributed the authorship of the *Shrimadbhagavad-Gita*, and who is worshipped as the eighth incarnation of Lord Vishnu, who come on the earth to restore the *Dharma*

Nanak Dev, the Guru : [1469-1539] was the first Sikh Guru and the founder of Sikhism, a social reformer and

		champion of communal harmony and human unity
Patel, Sardar Vallabhbhai	:	[1875, October 31–1950, December 15] was an Indian statesman and organizer, who played the vital role in the country's struggle for freedom and its unprecedented integration after the dawn of independence in 1947; was, and is, affectionately called as the *Sardar* and the *Iron Man of India*
Radhakrishnan, S.	:	[1888, September 5–1975, April 17] was an Indian philosopher and statesman, who served the country as its First Vice President [1952–62] and subsequently the Second President [1962–67]
Rama, the Lord	:	The hero of the epic *Ramayana*, who is regarded by Hindus as an ideal man and the king, and he is worshipped as the seventh incarnation of Lord Vishnu

Ruskin, John : [1819-1900] was a British thinker, a leading poet, an author and artist; his art and architecture-related essays were tremendously significant and influential in the Victorian and Edwardian eras

Saraswati, Swami Dayananda : [1824-1883] was a great *Vedic*-Hindu scholar, social reformer and the founder of the *Arya Samaj* [Society of Nobles] in 1875; was a believer in the infallible authority of the *Vedas* and it was he who for the first time gave the call for *Swarajya* in 1876, which was later furthered by Bal Gangadhar Tilak; was a supporter of equal rights for women; his gigantic contribution could be found in his unique work of translating the *Vedas* from Sanskrit into Hindi for the common man

Shradhanand, Swani : [1856-1926] was a leading *Arya Samajist*, an educationist and missionary to propagate the

		teachings of *Maharishi* Dayananda *Saraswati*; was the founder of the Gurukul Kangri University at Haridwar [now in Uttrakhand province of India], was also one of the leading figures to join the nationwide protest against the Rowlatt Act in 1919
Smut, JC	:	[1870-1950] Was a prominent South African and British Commonwealth statesman and a military general, who besides holding various cabinet posts, served as the Prime Minister of the Union of South Africa between 1919 and 1924 and again between 1939 and 1948, and who in most of his public life advocated segregation between the races and he was opposed to the unilateral enfranchisement of the black majority in South Africa
Shastri, Manohar Muni	:	[1951, December 20] is a known *Jainacharya* originally from Saurashtra, Gujarat [India]

Tolstoy, Leo	: [1828-1910] also known as Lev Nikolayevich Tolstoy, was a Russian writer widely regarded as one of the greatest of the European novelists; he was the author of *War and Peace*, *Anna Karenina*, and *The Kingdom of God is Within You*; he left a profound impact on people like Mahatma Gandhi and Martin Luther King Jr.
Tulsidas	: [1497-1623] was a great Hindu poet and saint, a social reformer and philosopher renowned for his devotion for Rama the Lord and composer of the epic *Ramacharitmanas*
Ulpian	: [170 – 223 AD] Gnaeus Domitius Annius Ulpianus, anglicized as Ulpian was an eminent Roman jurist of Tyrian ancestry
Yudhishthira	: The eldest of the *Pandavas* – son of King Pandu and Queen Kunti, was the King of Indraprastha and later of Hastinapur, was also the

leader of the *Pandavas* in the battle of Kurukshetra [*Mahabharata*], and was known as *Dharmaraja* –the righteous king or the king of the *Dharma*

*****

Glossary of Indian Terms

Akhand	: Undivided, whole
Ananda	: Pleasure, happiness, joy, delight
Arhata	: A spiritual practitioner who realizes certain high stages of attainment
Aryan	: Honourable, noble, one who belongs to Aryan race, excellent
Arya Samaj	: The society of nobles, a sect of reformist Hindus who are against idol worship, a movement founded by Swami Dayananda Saraswati in 1975
Asahayog	: Non-Cooperation
Atmavat Sarvabhuteshu	: Equality of vision
Asvikar	: Rejection, refusal, turning down, denying
Amaryaadit	: Unlimited
Bhagavata	: The adorable one
Brahman	: The One Who is the Supreme
Dharma	: Behaviour; deeds, duty, feeling, religious injunction

Gita, the	: The Song Celestial, highly philosophical verses laying emphasis on the selfless view of life and action
Harijan	: One belonging to untouchable class, a weekly started by Mahatma Gandhi early in the fourth decade of the Twentieth Century
Harijan	: Literally *Children of God*, a term coined by Mahatma Gandhi for untouchable in India
Harijan Sewak	: A Hindi weekly started by Mahatma Gandhi in the fourth decade of the Twentieth Century along with Harijan, another weekly in English
Hartal	: Strike, suspension of work as a mark of protest or mourning
Hind Swarajya	: Indian home rule, a book authored by Gandhi in first decade of the Twentieth Century
Karuna	: Compassion
Khadi	: Handspun hand-woven cloth
Mahatma	: Literally, high-souled person, a title bestowed on Gandhi by Rabindranath Tagore

Mandala	: A circle, division
Manusmriti	: The most important and earliest metrical work of the *Dharmashastra* textual tradition of *Vedic*-Hinduism, known in English as the *Laws of Manu*
Maulvi	: A title of respect applied to a learned Muslim
Metta	: Kindness, friendliness
Moksha	: Literally, release, liberation
Mukti	: Literally, release, liberation
Nirvana	: Literally, release, liberation
Nivriti	: Retirement, release
Parasparopgraho Jeevanam	: Souls rendering service to one-another
Parmodharma	: Religion in grandeur
Ramacharitmanas	: The Hindu epic [composed by Tulsidas] narrating the story of the abduction of Sita, wife of Lord Rama –the Prince of Ayodhya, by Ravana –the demon-king of Lanka, and her rescue after the conquest of Lanka by the army lead by Rama

		and the death of Ravaṇa at Rama's haṇd
Ramarajya	:	Divine Rule, the Kingdom of God; it is not a Hindu rule as Gandhi himself clarifies, ***"For me Rama and Rahim are one and the same deity; I acknowledge no other God but the one God of truth and righteousness, and whether Rama of my imagination ever lived or not on this earth, the ancient ideal of Ramarajya is undoubtedly one of true democracy in which the meanest citizen could be sure of swift justice without an elaborate and costly procedure, even the dog is described by the poet to have received justice under Ramarajya…Ramarajya of my dream ensures equal rights alike of prince and pauper"***
Rigveda	:	The first among the four *Vedas*, the sacred early Hindu scriptures
Rishi	:	A sage or seer, the most learned, a great scholar [a term denotes the composers of *Vedic* Hymns]

Sadhana	:	To achieve by work or devotion, to study, to accomplish, to learn
Samskara or sanskar	:	Instinct
Sanatana	:	The old
Sanskriti	:	Culture
Sarvodaya	:	Generally rise or development of all, one of the most important aspects of Gandhian philosophy
Satyagraha	:	Insistence on truth, resistance offered to uphold truth [a weapon popularized by Mahatma Gandhi during the Indian freedom stiruggle]
Shloka	:	A verse, couplet
Srimadbhagvadgita	:	The Song Celestial, highly philosophical verses laying emphasis on the selfless view of life and action
Sukta	:	A hymn
Sutra	:	Literally, a thread or line, which holds things together, rule, formula
Swami	:	An owner, proprietor, master, saint, lord, king, a title of the Supreme Being, popularly used for a religious teacher

Swarajya	: Self-rule, self-governance [espoused first of all by *Maharishi Dayananda Saraswati [1824-1883] then* by Bal Gangadhar Tilak [1856-1920] in the first decade of the Twentieth Century and later, concepts developed by Mahatma Gandhi to describe a stateless society in India free of foreign domination]
Upanishads	: Sacred ancient books of the Hindus, highly philosophical texts and early source of Hinduism – one hundred eight in number
Vedas	: The sacred early Hindu scriptures-four in number
Vedic	: Pertaining or belonging to or related with the *Vedas*, most sacred and ancient scriptures of the Hindus-four in number
Vishram	: Rest

*****

Index

B

C

D

E

F

G

H

I

J

K

L

M

N

O

S

T

U

V

W

Y

*****

"To me political power is not an end but one of the means of enabling people to better their condition in every department of life. Political power means capacity to regulate national life through national representatives." **-MK Gandhi**